FROM THE GROUND UP
A Plan to Build Your Christian Family

by Kenneth Kremer

Library of Congress Card 98-66987
Northwestern Publishing House
1250 N. 113th St., Milwaukee, WI 53226-3284
© 2000 by Northwestern Publishing House
Published 2000
Printed in the United States of America
ISBN 0-8100-0905-6

To Mom and Dad
with love, gratitude,
and deep affection.

ACKNOWLEDGMENTS

Lots of people have contributed to this book. Some have helped in ways of which I am not even aware. I am keenly aware of the contributions of others who offered encouragement along the way. Joel Gerlach said just the right things to give me confidence in the concept. Curtis Jahn and Owen Dorn supplied some badly needed direction. Joel Nelson, James Aderman, Brian Gerlach, Lisa Scheunemann, and Jean Lehninger provided honest and constructive readings of the manuscript. And I am especially grateful for the friendship of Lyle Albrecht. His literary perspective helped me remain objective throughout the writing.

In a personal way, this book represents the love and devotion of family. The support of my wife, Marlis, and my children and their families has been unwavering. The Spirit's working presence is evident in them too. They remain constant reminders to me that *"unless the LORD builds the house, its builders labor in vain"* (Psalm 127:1).

May the Lord's countenance shine brightly on all who helped bring this work to completion. And may these words bring glory, honor, and praise to the holy name of our great Lord and Savior.

FROM THE GROUND UP

PREFACE

Picture life without family. Hard to imagine, isn't it? Life begins in the home. Our earliest relationships are established there. Character is shaped in the family setting. Personalities formed. Values cultivated. Family members nurture one another, encourage one another, comfort one another, support one another, and provide peace and order for the good of all. In a bygone era people said, "Family gives us roots." Considering all the blessings family brings to us, life would be very different without one.

But the blessings of family are not always a given. Too many marriages are ludicrous caricatures of what God intended. Too many children grow up with no one to care for them or nurture them. Some have squandered the gift of family. Some have trashed it. To complicate matters, today's family contends with dangerous new economic pressures and social trends. Lifestyle has almost become a religion. The American home is adrift in a sea of change. Family is desperately in search of its center—something to be grounded on, a reason for existing.

God has set us apart. In his eyes we are to be special, unique. Our families are—or ought to be—different from the unbelieving families of the world. Christlike demeanors *declare the praises of him who called you out of darkness into his wonderful light*" (1 Peter 2:9). Yet the Christian family has not always met these challenges with distinction and resolve. Our lifestyles are often indistinguishable from the pagan families that surround us—our faith well camouflaged.

For some this book will serve as a call to repentance and reform. If your family has failed to live the life of a Christian household, be encouraged. It is never too late. Your home can become a place where hearts glow with the peace and joy that surpasses all human understanding.

But this book is aimed largely at the next generation of Christian home builders. If you are in your teens or twenties, you represent the Christian family of the 21st century. This book will help you review what being a Christian family really means. It will help you envision what the members of a Christian home do and say that sets them apart from families that don't live in the shadow of the cross. This book's purpose, then, is to define the Christian family—especially the spiritual activity of the Christian home.

If Christian homes are going to give people roots—the kind that will make their homes distinctively Christian—faith must be at the core of everyday life. Faith is at the heart of this book. The message is rooted deep in the soil of the gospel. To determine what distinguishes the Christian home from all others is to first consider what the Bible has to say about God's family.

Today's reader has a tendency to look to the bottom line. Frequently the reader demands, "Give me something practical." In a book like this, that is a tempting choice. I could have offered the familiar steps to follow, but I wanted something more. As Christians we must first grasp all that *God has done* for us before *we do* anything practical. Consequently, the discussion of what a Christian home can be will frequently lead us back to God's remarkable act of redemption. Our response follows: we build Christian families empowered by the rich grace of God.

The home-builder metaphor illustrates how the faith of individuals takes shape within the family setting. God provides the plan, the resources, and the energy for building the Christian home. The blueprint we follow is God's. His building materials are familiar: a bedrock foundation, a well for water, lighting considerations, supporting beams.

Next comes the work! Building a new home is never a small undertaking. We approach it with anticipation, confidence, enthusiasm, and excitement. But because it is God's work, we also approach it with a healthy dose of fear and trembling. And then, we leave the results up to the contractor.

As you build, you will be able to watch the members of your household grow. You will see them enjoying vibrant, loving relationships with one another. And family life will become an exciting adventure as you share your faith in Jesus with one another. More important, your home building experience will prepare you and the members of your family for moving into your eternal home, where there will be rest from your labors forever.

∽ A PARABLE ∽

There once lived a fine, Christian young man who married and started a family of his own. He loved his wife. They began their life together in God's house before his altar. Soon God blessed their marriage with children, whom the man loved with a deep affection.

In the spring of their lives, the man worked very hard. He wanted to provide a good home for his family. He enjoyed being a loyal companion to his wife and a kind father to his children. Each day was an opportunity he seized eagerly. Occasionally he would take his wife and children to God's house, but more often than not, he chose to stay at home with his family.

In time the man saved enough money to build a new house—a haven, safe from wild animals and thieves. He worked hard building a comfortable place to live. The rooms were large and inviting. The walls were decorated with wonderful textures and cheerful colors. And the floors were covered with a thick, soft carpet.

Soon many other people settled in the same valley. The choices for friends, schools, shopping, and jobs multiplied. The man's family rubbed elbows with people from many different cultures and lifestyles. His children seemed to thrive on the freedom to shape themselves without restraint or boundaries. And the man thought to himself, "This is good. Each of my children can now truly become his own person and create his own destiny." The man and his family were busy every moment and had no time to return to God's house. What they had learned slowly became only a nostalgic memory.

As the leaves turned to orange, the man noticed a draft wafting through the hallways. "This will never do," he thought. "Winter will soon be upon us. If I do not insulate against the cold, we will freeze." So the man weather-stripped all the doors and windows. Then he laid a thick layer of insulation in the attic.

Soon the gales of November whistled in from the north. The house was still not airtight. The cold crept in under the floorboards and through the walls. The man's diligent efforts had provided many things for his wife and family, but nothing he did could take the chill from his house.

His family seemed happy, but the man was troubled. He felt alone. His children talked less and less with one another. He wondered what good a family was if its members stopped laughing together and working together. He began to search for a way to rekindle the warmth and love he had known in the spring of his life.

The man invited his family to gather every day to talk about their lives and to share their joys and sorrows, but no one came. It was as though the cold had numbed their spirits and frozen their hearts. The children were too busy to come. His wife could not stop even to consider how she missed the warm love of their early days. Every day became like the one before.

The December storms grew fierce, but nothing changed. Soon blizzards came. The man sought advice from every expert he could imagine. They advised him on every problem he shared. Again and again he would return to his family to try some new technique or strategy, but whatever he tried was only a temporary fix. The cold remained and after a time seemed to grow worse.

The days of raging blizzards turned into weeks of sub-zero temperatures. The man was bewildered. He wondered how he might have built his home differently.

Then, one bitter January morning, the man awoke to find himself alone. A note addressed "Dear Father" lay on the kitchen table. It said, "We've gone to look for a house with a fire burning in the hearth." ∞

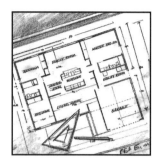

1. THE RIGHT ARCHITECT!

Christian home building takes effort and concentration. It takes time and commitment. Building a spiritual home with a warm fire burning in the hearth is one of the most important things any of us will ever do in our lifetime. Such effort promises many blessings. But the immensity and intensity of the work can never be overlooked.

So, where does a novice builder like yourself begin? Is there anyone you can ask to help you build? If you are like most people, you need help building a home. You need someone with experience and knowledge about home building. The first thing is to find a reliable architect who can help you develop plans and bring your dream into reality.

Of course, we are talking about building a Christian family— a home—not just building a wood and plaster house. Who better to ask for help than the One who made you and brought you together as husband and wife? The Lord is deeply interested in you, your spouse, and your children. He will remain there with you on-site. He will be with you throughout the building experience. He's the right choice.

THE PERFECT FAMILY?

Do you ever fantasize about having the perfect family? Most of us spend a lifetime trying to live that dream. We can even picture it: a good job, a cozy home with a garden, an attic full of memories, happy times, new beginnings with children and grandchildren, and a graceful exit. We celebrate our dreams together with the people who mean the most to us.

Not long ago I spent a year's worth of spare time and free weekends remodeling our basement. It had become a dark, spooky place for storing memories and the junk memorabilia that is supposed to preserve them. My plan was to turn it into a comfortable living area. Our two children had grown to adulthood and moved out of state. They would need a place to stay whenever they came for a visit.

We couldn't afford to hire an architect and contractor for the project, so I decided to have a try at home construction myself. It was my first real experience with plumb lines, Sheetrock, headers, and bathroom plumbing. The experience turned out to be very worthwhile.

The project grew in scope, and it soon became an obsession. As it neared completion, I began to realize that my dream had a lot more to do with keeping my family together than it had to do with tile inlays or joint compound. I was still working on my family fantasy.

Some of us will come closer to achieving our dream than others. Every now and then we pause in the harsh light of life's realities to review our progress. Taking a family inventory is not that complicated. Family boils down to just a few essentials. Success or failure is almost always determined by the kind of relationships family members enjoy. Sometimes such self-evaluation can be unbearably painful, but it is always instructive.

Relationships are the Bible's forte. That's the place to go if you really want to understand the Christian home. The Bible's picture of a healthy, godly household includes plenty of relational stuff. It teaches what commitment means. It tells us how to live together in harmony. It shows us how important it is for us to take an interest in one another's lives. It encourages us to share our personal faith and trust in Jesus with one another.

The things the Bible has to say about our relationships with one another are very important. But they are, at least in one sense, a secondary message. The Bible is even more concerned with telling us about our eternal home and our relationship with our heavenly Father.

The Bible describes our relationship with God as a family relationship. He is our Father, and we are his children. Good things like joy, peace, love, and honor—things that we want in our relationships with one another on earth—have their origin in our heavenly Father's relationship with us. The Christian home builder will first want to study this relationship.

Life on our planet began with the kind of ideal household you and I dream of. The human family was once perfectly happy. Our ancestral parents walked in the garden and talked with their Father-Creator daily. The place was Eden, and it was theirs to do with as they wished, as long as they honored their Creator's dominion over them.

They failed. And their disobedience cost them their claim to the only piece of real estate that mattered—the place where they could be together with their Maker. The perfect family had been irreparably shattered.

The disobedience of Adam and Eve ruined the open and loving relationship they once had with their Creator. Now they doubted God and mistrusted him. *Self* intruded into their perfect understanding of his holy will. In fact, self became their new focus in life. They knew hatred for the first time. And their own Father-Creator was the object of their hatred. Shame replaced joy. Fear supplanted security. They felt guilt and sought to avoid responsibility for their own failure. Gone were the quiet walks together. The conversations with God that had breathed spiritual life into their relationship became terrifying.

The breach was so terrible that Adam and Eve tried to hide. They were ashamed. They had dishonored their Father. It was their fault that his house was in disorder, cold and empty. They were to blame. And they were properly terrified to face his eternal anger. Life without the Father's loving approval was simply not worth enduring.

Their disobedience destroyed other relationships too. God had entrusted all of his created world into Adam's care and keeping. At first, the relationship between man and the natural world was perfectly harmonious. But when Adam and Eve disobeyed God, as part of their punishment, nature challenged its caretaker. Life became a struggle to survive. Worse, man's own self-interest now often led him to abuse the natural world. It all played out so tragically. Greed, wanton wastefulness, and neglect drove human decisions. And the planet's magnificent natural resources suffered as a result.

Family life became hopelessly entangled in the daily struggle to eke out a living. There were mouths to feed. Yet crops would fail because of blights or droughts. Tools would break or rust. Clothing would wear out. Flocks and herds would require constant attention and protection. Floods, earthquakes, and terrible winds would tear down buildings. Everything would deteriorate, including bodies that would wear out under the burden of labor, disease, and the aging process.

Human relationships also ceased to be peaceful and harmonious. They became uncharted paths through a treacherous swamp of guilt, jealousy, greed, fear, finger-pointing, lust, deceit, hatred, and a desire to dominate. Earth's first family, now living under the rule of sin, suffered a heartache that has been repeated millions of times since. Stirred by envy, Eve's firstborn child, Cain, murdered his younger brother, Abel. The human, sin-driven heart had even turned against members of its own family. Brother against brother. Sister against sister. Husbands and wives, parents and children, torn apart.

The infection extended beyond the nuclear family. Tribes went to war with neighboring tribes for the same wicked, self-serving reasons. Nor was this self-destructive behavior restricted to one generation. Each generation passed on the same characteristics to the succeeding one. Examples of cruelty, deceit, and bloodshed not only fill the newspapers of our society, but they also fill the pages of every history book. One civilization overran another. Cultures clashed and crashed under the burden of corruption and greed. Government malfunctioned and governed with little regard for those who were under its thumb. Despots and tyrants ruled with ruthless force. Bigotry and prejudice at times dominated policy. And the whole human family suffered under the weight of perversion and injustice.

> **Human relationships . . . became uncharted paths through a treacherous swamp of guilt, jealousy, greed, fear, finger-pointing, lust, deceit, hatred, and a desire to dominate.**

Such distortions begin in the human heart. Our personal demons become legion. All too often our hearts slip down into the ooze of lust, hatred, resentment, pride, deceit, and vanity. Humanity becomes paralyzed by indecision and fear, traumatized by self-abuse and emotional blood-letting, beaten down by loneliness and self-pity.

We are determined to be in charge of our lives—to make our own way. We've lost the image of our Creator. Tormented by sin, we don't have the spiritual resources to make even a single righteous decision. On our own we are hopeless failures. And deep down, where a hint of the truth still lingers, we know what pathetic creatures we have become. So we hate even ourselves.

Sin has stripped us of every meaningful relationship. There is no way to escape this fact. We are as much at war with our Creator as Adam and Eve were. Our conflict with God has spread to conflict with nature, with one another, and even with self. What a hopeless, lonely, useless existence! What a way to live, if you can even call that living! God created us to relate wonderfully with him and others, yet we are doomed to isolation on every front by our own wicked self-will.

No wonder the perfect family seems like such an empty promise! Its precious relationships have been twisted, tortured, distorted, and perverted. No wonder we are physically, emotionally, socially, and spiritually dysfunctional! Sin envelopes us, attacks us, overpowers us, and destroys us. It lives inside our hearts. Because of it, the whole human family writhes in hopelessness and despair. We have lost our identity. Our souls have forgotten our reason for being. Our legacy consists of nothing more than a lonely, desperate no-man's land—a spiritual island without a shred of hope for a meaningful future.

DIVINE BUILDER

Even for the best of families, sin is a huge problem. I'm proud of my family. But I also cringe at the terrible mistakes we have made along the way. We've hurt one another, disappointed one another, betrayed, used, and abused one another. By most standards we might be described as a normal, healthy, functional Christian family. But *normal* by the standards of this world is also *sinful*. My home has a dark side. And I'm sure yours does too. We go to great lengths to conceal that fact from our public. But it's true. Sin is always there lurking in the background, undermining our relationships.

Even more tragic, sin has dashed any hope we might have of patching up our relationship with our heavenly Father. Left to us and our unholy schemes, a reconciliation with heaven is a foolish proposition. Nothing we do or say could ever undo the damage. We have no resources for dealing with the collapse of our relationship with God. We don't even have the inclination. Sin makes us look upon God as the enemy. Our natural instinct is to battle God every step of the way. He says, "This is what I want for you." We say, "No! I'll go my own way." We run in the opposite direction in the same way that Adam and Eve did, filled with shame and terror, puffed up with pride and conceit.

Look around. How successful have we been at resolving the hatred between family members? Look further into the global village. How well have we been able to reconstruct the rifts between tribes, or races, or nations? To believe that the human race has somehow matured enough to change all this by ourselves is pure delusion. How foolish! We are no closer to patching up our rotten relationships today than were our ancestors thousands of years ago. Not with one another. Not within our own hearts. And certainly not with God. If such a place where man and his Maker can be together again exists, it would take an act of God to find it.

And that is exactly what has happened. The spiritual home we long for exists in the heart of the Creator. He restores our shattered relationships. He understands relationships. He should; he created them. He alone has the resources powerful enough to heal them.

On our own the search for advice on how to heal our relationships with one another and with our Maker would be pointless. Only our heavenly Father has what we so desperately need. His love mended our broken relationship with him, and it is also the salve to heal our wounds and repair our relationships. It's not natural to seek God as the architect and contractor for family life. We naturally think we can do it on our own, and so we turn to every other source for advice. But our heavenly Father has known what we need all along and offers it to us without cost. Imagine such a builder, who will design and help you construct your Christian home and not charge you a fee. He will take his pleasure in seeing you succeed and even give you all you need to succeed.

God alone has the resources powerful enough to heal our shattered relationships.

THE CONTRACTOR'S RECORD

If you want good work done, you need a reliable contractor. I have friends who decided to build a home and then had all kinds of trouble with the contractor. In fact, the contractor went bankrupt and brought them more than a little frustration and difficulty. We are building a Christian home, and we want the best. We don't want to be left with a half-completed house or worse. A good rule of thumb in building is to check the references of the contractor and look at the work he has done for others.

Of all the relationships shattered by man's rebellion, one survives, unscathed and intact. The Creator's love for his fallen creatures endures. Granted, that relationship is one-sided. The creature despises the Creator, and that hurts God deeply. Yet the Father still loves the wayward children of his creation. Since sin makes it impossible for us to relate to him, he relates to us. He has left a wonderful record of his past work. Let's explore it a bit.

The people of Israel spent 430 years in Egypt. At first their sojourn in Egypt helped them survive starvation. Over those years the Pharaoh eventually made them slaves and even sought to destroy all their male children. It was time for God to act, so he called Moses to deliver them from their captors. Before sending Moses off on his mission, God revealed who he is. *"God said to Moses, 'I AM WHO I AM. This is what you are to say to the Israelites: "I AM has sent me to you"'"* (Exodus 3:14). What a wonderful name! God lives in the present, I AM. He is not I was nor I will be, but I AM.

His people could not rescue themselves. They were helpless. God acted to deliver them. Not only did I AM take the lead in delivering his people, he traveled the journey with them, sharing every inch of the desert road. His compassion was self-evident as I AM lived among the sojourners. As they moved from place to place, pitching their tents along the way, so did I AM. He, the Lord I AM, lived at the center of their encampment. He knew their living conditions. I AM was at the heart of their culture, their law, their art, their music, their seasonal celebrations, their daily activities. He sustained them on manna and quail. He resided there in a pillar of cloud by day and a pillar of fire by night. He was really, physically present among them. I AM, the God of great compassion, extended himself into man's world—the world of sin that had rejected its Creator.

God's real presence in the world of sinners is a theme repeated again and again throughout the Old Testament. I AM was always there with his people, even when they turned their backs on him.

When the future of God's people seemed bleakest, the Lord sent a prophet named Isaiah to tell the faithful about a Man of God who would be called Immanuel. *Immanuel* means "God with us." Isaiah's description, rendered seven centuries before the birth of Christ, spoke in astounding detail of Jesus' life and death. And Isaiah's prophetic words were echoed by others.

God waited for the perfect moment. When the timing was right, the LORD, I AM, left heaven's majestic throne. He entered our world, as all humans do, in a family way, through a birth canal. Of this electric moment in history, Matthew later wrote, *"All this took place to fulfill what the Lord had said through the prophet: 'The virgin will be with child and will give birth to a son, and they will call him Immanuel'—which means, 'God with us'"* (Matthew 1:22,23).

The Lord God—the I AM of the Old Testament—had joined the human race. He would experience hunger and need to eat. He would feel pain and sadness. He would know thirst. He would tire, as other people tire. He would bleed. And he would die. I AM was Immanuel, "God with us," in the flesh.

Matthew's gospel ends with what may have been the last words that our Immanuel spoke on earth. His tender words reassuringly echoed both Moses and Isaiah: *"Surely I am with you always, to the very end of the age"* (Matthew 28:20).

Jesus is at the center of everything that happens in the daily life of a Christian household.

Isn't this the One you want to help you build your home? Jesus is present in your home, just as he promised. He is at the center of everything that happens in your daily life. He blesses the members of your household whenever and wherever you come together in his name. He eats with you, sleeps with you, laughs with you, cries with you. He is at the heart of your family culture, your family law, and your family celebrations. The pictures of him that hang on your walls remind you that he is there. So does the Bible on your kitchen table and the cross in your living room. That cross reminds you of his cross—of his forgiveness. It's the glue that holds your family together. It is also the energy that sends family members on their separate ways each new day.

He lives in your home because he resides in your individual hearts. You know he is there because you talk about him with one another. You build your spiritual home with Jesus, in Jesus' name, and around the power of Jesus' holy Word. You are healed in his forgiveness and are assured of life eternal in his holy supper. There, in that communion, you are reminded that he is really *present with you.*

Try to define the Christian home in a single word, and the word would have to be *Jesus,* I AM's Son, *God with us.* He is what distinguishes the Christian family from all others.

BUILDING YOUR HOUSE OF GOD

God led his people out of Egypt, but they demonstrated the rebellion in their hearts. Again and again they complained about God and his leader, Moses. They even chose to hold a worship festival dedicated to a golden calf at the very foot of the mountain where I AM appeared to them. It was a sad story.

But God did not abandon them. After their rebellion, God revealed even more about himself. To Moses, God revealed himself: *"The* LORD, *the* LORD, *the compassionate and gracious God, slow to anger, abounding in love and faithfulness, maintaining love to thousands, and forgiving wickedness, rebellion and sin"* (Exodus 34:6,7).

Are you still wondering about letting God be the contractor for your home? Those words should settle things. But you still may have some questions. We can look at another example of what the Lord can do. It's the story of two brothers, Jacob and Esau (Genesis 27–33). They were twins but grew up with much different interests. Esau didn't care much about domestic matters. He directed his energy to the adventurous life of a hunter. Jacob seems to have been a homebody. And he was a shrewd opportunist.

Esau was born first and was, therefore, the heir apparent. But one day he traded his birthright to Jacob for a serving of stew. It seemed like an innocent enough matter. Yet Esau's choice exposed a cavalier attitude toward something very sacred.

The relationship between the brothers slipped further toward disaster when Rebekah, their mother, stepped between Esau and his father, Isaac. She conspired with Jacob to deceive Isaac into formally blessing Jacob with the birthright. The deception succeeded in gaining Jacob the birthright, but it also set the family on the edge of catastrophe.

Esau was consumed by hatred toward his brother. Young Jacob fled for his life. Alone, heartsick, estranged from his family, Jacob hit bottom.

Then, in the cold darkness of Jacob's own wicked making, God came to him in a dream. In it Jacob saw a stairway that stretched from heaven to earth. Angels marched in both directions, walking down the stairway to where Jacob was and also walking upward toward God. I AM stood above it all. The Lord told Jacob he would one day lead Jacob safely back to the land of promise: *"I am with you and will watch over you wherever you go, and I will bring you back to this land. I will not leave you until I have done what I have promised you"* (Genesis 28:15).

Now Jacob knew that God had not abandoned him. In spite of all the terrible crimes he had committed against the members of his own family, God still loved him. A father unable to restore Jacob to full membership in his divine family could never make such a promise. The stairway dream was Jacob's gospel. The Lord had provided the healing Jacob needed. He had dealt with Jacob's guilt and restored Jacob to his divine family.

Every member of every family needs the same compassion, forgiveness, and love.

Jacob marked the spot of his vision with the same stone that he had used as a pillow the night before. He consecrated the ground, pouring oil on the stone. Then he named the place Bethel—"house of God." Here he learned of the heavenly Father's forgiveness. Because of God's promise, Jacob's most vital relationship was always safe and secure. Jacob went on from that place to build his house with the Lord. He still stumbled along the way. There was still jealousy, bitterness, and family strife, but with the Lord his house took shape and grew.

The LORD, I AM, demonstrated compassion, forgiveness, and love for Jacob. Every member of every family needs the same compassion, forgiveness, and love. God is love. Such love embraces us when our actions hurl our own families to the edge of disaster. Such love sets down the patterns we need to be compassionate, forgiving, and loving to the members of our families. Finally, such love prompts us to be like our heavenly Father: to show kindness when someone in our family is unkind, to forgive when we are hurt, and to love even when our families don't show us the love we expect.

We'll need help to do all that. It's a very tall order. God can do it. He's the helper we need.

BUILDING OBJECTIVES:

- To talk with one another about your personal relationships.

- To talk daily about sin's tragic consequences and about the forgiveness that is yours in Christ Jesus.

- To teach your children that Jesus is really and always present with us.

- To appreciate the strength we receive from partaking of the Lord's Supper regularly.

BUILDING BLOCKS

- Read Genesis 2:18-24. Ask each member of your family (even if that is only you and your spouse) to say at least one thing the passage says about family and marriage.

- Read Genesis 4:1-16. Discuss with your family why Cain killed his brother. Ask whether Cain's attitude exists in families today.

- In Exodus 34:6 God tells us he is compassionate, merciful, patient, always faithful, and ready to forgive. We are to be like God and possess these qualities. Why are they valuable for your family? Discuss how each member of your family can demonstrate these qualities.

- Encourage the confirmed members of your family to be strengthened regularly by receiving the Lord's Supper.

2. DEEP WELL

You have chosen a good contractor—the best. Now it's time to think about a few other things. Every house needs water. People build where there is an abundant supply. Water is vital to sustaining life. We need water for drinking, cooking, bathing, and washing clothes.

Human beings cannot survive without water. Waste produced by our bodies contains deadly toxins. The liquids we drink flush dangerous poisons out through our kidneys. Without this cleansing, the body's systems would quickly shut down.

Water is also essential to our biological air-conditioning system. It helps us maintain a constant temperature. When we become overheated, perspiration on the skin evaporates, drawing heat away from the body. In cold weather we don't need to sweat. Instead, the warmth generated by our bodies is pumped through the bloodstream to keep the body's temperature at a constant 98.6° Fahrenheit. It all needs the simple liquid compound H_2O.

Water is also important for removing dirt. We bathe regularly to keep microscopic particles and organisms from causing infection.

Water is a basic physical need. But we have a need for spiritual refreshment and renewal too. Our souls depend on a spiritual kind of water. God himself is the only source for this *water of life*. Without a steady stream of his spiritual blessings, our souls are as good as dead.

Christian families have access to an endless supply of this divine water. It gives them new life here on earth, sustaining their faith in God's promises for eternity. The members of a Christian household will want to return to this refreshing, life-giving fountain often.

Without a steady stream of God's spiritual blessings, our souls are as good as dead.

LIVING LAKES AND DEAD SEAS

A few years ago, my wife and I toured the Holy Land. Our first impression has been a lasting impression: the geography of the land God promised to Abraham, Isaac, Jacob, and their descendants is no accident. The Holy Land is a land of dramatic contrasts. In the fertile northern valleys, lush crops of fruits and vegetables grow in abundance. They depend upon predictable, annual rainfalls during the late winter and early spring.

But the northern green acreage gives way quickly to another landscape far more bleak and brutal. This part of Israel appears inhospitable. In the Judean hills south and east of Jerusalem, for example, one encounters only an occasional Bedouin troop with their flocks. The land is simply too harsh to support a larger population.

As if the difference in terrain itself were not enough, two landlocked bodies of water punctuate the contrast. In the north lies the Sea of Galilee, placid and beautiful. Its waters are fed by the snowy slopes of Mount Hermon. About 65 miles to the south, some 1,300 feet below sea level, is the Dead Sea—forbidding, lifeless. The two are connected by a narrow ribbon of river called the

Jordan. It flows north to south. Fresh waters from the Sea of Galilee end up in the Dead Sea.

The Sea of Galilee brings life to the farming communities and fishing villages that surround it. Jesus grew up near the Sea of Galilee. In the early months of his ministry, Jesus and his disciples spent many hours along its inviting shores.

The Dead Sea and everything around it is just as its name implies. The water's salt content makes it impossible for plants and animals to live here. Vistas along the Dead Sea leave tourists with an eerie, otherworldly impression. It's not difficult to imagine you are marooned on another planet.

The spiritual significance of these two dramatically different bodies of water is not lost on the people who live there. Israelis today speak of "living water" and "dead water." They say, "Living water gives and keeps on giving; dead water cannot give." That's an instructive insight—one worthy of some thought.

Living water gives and keeps on giving. Dead water cannot give.

Have you ever encouraged someone to drive carefully, or have you ever been concerned for someone's health? Of course you have. Can you think of anything more valuable to you or the members of your family than life itself? Who would dare to be reckless with life or cavalier about its value? Yet we sometimes treat spiritual life with that attitude. And when we do, we are in great peril. Such an attitude can be deadly. The implications are long-term. In fact, the implications are eternal and absolute. We must do something to find this life-giving water for ourselves and our families.

But there is a problem here—another terrible consequence of sin. When it comes to spiritual life, we are dead from the moment of our own conception. In effect, our souls are stillborn. Sin is a congenital spiritual condition—a birth defect. We have no natural appreciation for the life of our souls or the God who promises to give us spiritual life. Like the Dead Sea, in spiritual terms, we cannot give—not to one another or to the God who created us.

We are spiritually dead. We cannot come to God. We cannot find the water of life by our intelligent searching or our painstaking effort. We are dead.

We sometimes foolishly imagine that we can somehow charm our Creator. We think that he will give us the water of life because we perform his works or because we are better than the "scum of society." But he's not interested in having a relationship with spiritual zombies. Dead is dead. Dead water cannot give. And our Creator-God is a God of life and of giving.

How heartsickening! Because we are dead, we cannot appear in our own Father's presence. He is life; we are death. We are trapped. We can do nothing to please him. Nothing we say can win his favor. And yet, he is the Author of life; without his sustaining love, we remain dead water, unable to give.

But our heavenly Father changes us. He gives us life when he comes to us in the gospel and changes our dead hearts to living ones. The miracle is as dramatic as the difference between the Dead Sea and the Sea of Galilee. We were dead like the Dead Sea; God made us alive like the Sea of Galilee. We could not come to God; he came to us. He made us his children when he gave us faith in Jesus.

SWEET WATER

I was eight years old when I encountered my first dead body. I remember the day as though I were still living it today. It was at my grandfather's funeral. I remember the expressions on the faces of the grown-ups. Oddly, I cannot recall any deep-felt sadness of my own. I understood he was in heaven with Jesus. But I vividly remember a sense of shock over the finality and absoluteness of death. The sight of his lifeless body hit me with the force of a sledgehammer. I knew instantly that he would never play with me again, read a book to me, or tickle me lovingly. But I wasn't worried about him. It was my life that concerned me. I knew that I didn't want to be dead like my grandpa. Not for a long time. Maybe not ever.

There is no virtue in being dead. And yet that is exactly what we deserve. God's perfect sense of justice cannot dismiss sin; sin will be punished. If you need proof, witness the Lord's terrible anger unleashed in the great flood. Except for a handful of people, the Almighty destroyed the earth because of human wickedness. And it was justly deserved. Sinners rightly have it coming. We deserve to spend eternity drowning in the hellhole of perpetual hate, separated from God and his love.

But Noah and seven members of his family were saved. They built an ark, according to God's precise instruction. They believed God's words. Their survival gives us hope.

There is a kind of baptism here in Scripture's record of the great deluge. The story of Noah's ark pictures God as he really is. On one hand, his justice demands that sin be punished. The wicked were washed clean off the face of the earth. On the other hand, his love intervenes on behalf of sinners. Thus Noah and his family were spared.

Our hopeless situation calls for a miracle of the highest order—divine intervention. We need to be washed clean, purified, and renewed if we are going to avoid God's judgment. Sin must be thoroughly removed. And the vacuum must be filled with a right-eousness so perfect that God will smile approvingly. The spiritually dead must be brought back to life, reborn to life, not death.

But *dead water cannot give.* It especially cannot give life. So living water must give instead. And the invaluable gift that the living water gives is the precious gift of life itself. Only the Giver of life is capable of giving it. First, God sent his precious Son to take the place of all humanity and suffer the consequences of our sins. By his act God has removed sin thoroughly and completely. Second, the Son of God, Jesus, has given all humanity the perfect righteous-ness God demands. Because of the suffering, death, and resurrection of Jesus, God declares the world righteous—perfectly righteous.

The living water once cried out from a cross, "I am thirsty," as he poured out every drop of his own life so that we might live.

God has demonstrated the same almighty power in us as he exercised in Noah's day. He has washed us clean. He has removed our sin and given us new life. Sin's deadly legacy was buried in the grave when Jesus' own lifeless body was laid to rest. His resurrection is our new life and the hope of life to come. We are indeed born again to life, not of an earthly father and mother, but of God himself. Jesus is the never-ending fountain, a bottomless well of life-giving water. With Jesus we have life. Without him we remain *dead water*. A Christian family—one that actually enjoys life as God intended— cannot live without Christ. It's an impossible contradiction.

Dead water cannot give, so Jesus gave what we could not. The living water once cried out from a cross, "I am thirsty," as he poured out every drop of his own life so that we might live. Dead water offends the Author of life. Dead water is unable to offer anything of value to a demanding, perfect Father. The living water— Jesus referred to himself as living water to the woman at Jacob's well—pleased the Father in every detail of his work.

Our baptism is tied to Jesus. Its promises for life are wrapped around Jesus' life, death, and resurrection. Our sins are washed away forever in the cleansing action of the blood he shed on Calvary. His powerful Word assures us of his never-ending fountain of forgiveness. Our dead past is behind us. We have joined the ranks of the living. As such, we can claim our rightful place in God's eternal family.

NEW AND IMPROVED

If contemporary life in America is anything, it is hurried. One contributing factor to our hurried lifestyle is our obsession with *newness*. My family is no exception. We recently became a two computer household. Now we argue the merits of PCs versus Macs with the rest of the digital universe. We buy the latest in new products. We enjoy using the most up-to-date technology. We watch for new trends, new twists to global happenings, new issues, new styles, new philosophies, new creature comforts, and new ideas.

Old things have a habit of wearing out. Perhaps our obsession for newness has something to do with our disappointment with oldness. Old machines rust. Old books become brittle. Old buildings weaken. Old bodies become frail. Eventually anything old will be put on the side, sent to pasture, thrown in the trash heap, or just plain forgotten.

If your home is anything like mine, you're experiencing the same sensation of being relentlessly driven toward whatever it is that comes next. It's a helpless feeling. But we get caught up in the flow. We sense a movement—a kind of momentum—and the frenetic chase is on. We hurry about, desperately searching for something— anything—that will give real and lasting meaning to our lives. The hope is that something *new* will come along to finally bring our search to an end.

There isn't much reason to be optimistic that this hurried feeling will end anytime soon. Sin has taken away our energy for resisting it. If *dead water* can't do much about giving, it can't do much about being old and useless either. It simply doesn't have the resources for inventing the one thing that will put an end to the search.

Renewal is our only hope. And God has done that too for us. In Jesus we have become *new creatures.* And, in the newness of our life in him, we are completely given over to serving him as our *new* Lord. Satan doesn't rule us anymore; Jesus is the *new* master of our lives.

For the people of the Old Testament, bathing and washing was more than just a social custom. Many of the ritual washing ceremonies were part of the Levitical laws. God had set these laws before his people so they would never forget their spiritual condition. Cups, pitchers, and kettles, for example, were not to be used in temple rites unless they had been purified. Once they were cleansed for temple use, they could no longer be used in any other capacity. The ritual washing made them holy, suitable only for serving the Lord.

That is what God has done for us. Jesus' blood has washed us clean, made us suitable for temple service. And in that cleansing, we are fully prepared for serving him. The term for such cleansing is *sanctification*. Your life—that is, your *new*, sanctified life in Christ—is the proof that you have been called into his family. God's work in your heart is a kind of down payment on the eternal promises of God. You are his. He has separated you for his service. You will also be with him eternally.

We were destined for hell: adulterers, idolaters, liars, cheats, tax evaders, sexual perverts, thieves, drunkards, slanderers, swindlers. Our anger, deceit, selfishness, greed, and pride clearly indicate that we failed to meet God's holy standards. Jesus changed that. In our new lives, rooted in Jesus' forgiveness, we are reborn in the image of the Creator. We become like the living water. In Jesus we are able to do and say good things that will please our heavenly Father.

As new creatures we can be patient and loving with one another, as Jesus was patient with us. As new creatures we can put the needs of others ahead of our own needs. In the newness of Christ, our conversations can reflect his love, our actions can take on the same appearance as Christ's actions. The living water of God's forgiveness has transformed us into living water—water that is able to give. In spiritual terms we look and act like Jesus. We are from the same spiritual family. We wear his goodness. We are alive and filled to overflowing with a new life.

> **One contributing factor to our hurried lifestyle is our obsession with newness.**

REMEMBER YOUR BAPTISM

My wife waded waist-deep into the muddy Jordan River to collect water in soft-drink bottles. Later we sealed the water in tiny vials and gave them to friends and family as momentos of our trip to the Holy Land.

A few weeks after our return to the States, our first grandchild was born. She was several weeks premature. Her father baptized her in the hospital. He used a vial of our Jordan River water. We understand that it's God's Word, not the location from which the water is drawn, that gives Baptism its power. Still, using this water from the Jordan River seemed a fitting way to help us remember this moment's significance.

Jesus instructed his followers to baptize all nations. The members of our own households are, of course, included under the umbrella of that commission. Christian parents want, for themselves and for their children, all the spiritual blessings that Baptism has to offer. Those blessings include God's assurance of the forgiveness of sins and his promise of eternal life in heaven.

But while we remain here on earth, we suffer from a kind of spiritual Alzheimer's Disease—another consequence of sin. We forget. We become distracted. We take the remarkable blessings of Baptism for granted. We lose track of our spiritual needs and the resources God has given us to address those spiritual needs.

God, who has thankfully forgotten our sins, doesn't want us ever to forget what he has done. The good news of the Bible is that God has done everything necessary for us to have a relationship with him. The Bible tells that story over and over. We call it the gospel. This gospel is a dynamic, on-going power in the lives of God's people. As long as we continue to breathe, the gospel moves us, shapes us, changes us, and challenges us. It's working in your heart right now. And for that reason, it deserves our constant attention and consideration. We think about it, pray about it, and talk about it. God's work of redeeming us is such an unexpected joy in our lives, it deserves never to be forgotten.

The message that God loves me, a sinner, is so undeserved, and thus unexpected, that it is remarkably fresh and new every time I hear it.

Baptism is a gospel proclamation. In Baptism God declares that we belong to his family from that moment on into eternity. Baptism actually washes away our sins and gives us all the blessings of life. What heartwarming, surprising news! When the members of a family daily remember their baptisms, the hurried scramble for newness can be put to rest. In Baptism we have everything God has to offer: a full and free pardon from our sin, reconciliation with the Father in heaven, the hope of future life there with him, and a meaningful and purposeful life here on earth.

The search is over. What more could anyone want or need? The message that God loves us sinners is so unexpected and so undeserved that it is fresh and new every time we hear it. When we reassure one another of God's love by remembering our baptisms, our earthly concerns become insignificant. Compared with the joy of knowing that we belong to God's family, the problems of this life seem unimportant.

Baptism marks the moment when a Christian's life really begins. Christian families need to find ways to celebrate its powerful significance in their lives. We need to remember the fullness of the life this living water has given us. The Christian home builder builds wisely by looking for daily opportunities to quench the thirst of family members with this remarkable living water.

BUILDING OBJECTIVES:

- To appreciate the gift of physical life and the significance of physical death.

- To remember that spiritual life and death have absolute and eternal implications.

- To celebrate Baptism and talk about its blessings often.

- To consider salvation in Christ Jesus to be a new and exciting gift every day.

- To treat God's boundless love as an unexpected surprise.

BUILDING BLOCKS

- Celebrate Baptism. Locate certificates or pictures of the baptisms of family members; read and talk about the day, the people who were present, and what God did in their baptisms.

- Review what Luther's Small Catechism says about Baptism. Read that part of the catechism aloud with your family.

- Baptism begins a new life, but life will never be perfect until we enter heaven. Read the Meaning of Baptism from Luther's Small Catechism. (It is also on page 12 of *Christian Worship*: "Baptism means . . .") Discuss how a new person who desires to live as God asks can daily arise in our hearts.

- Read Titus 3:3-8. Discuss with one another what the passage means to you. Each member of the family may select a few words from the passage and make a comment about what they mean.

3. SOLID FOUNDATION

From the stone that pillowed Jacob's head at Bethel to the two tablets containing God's law, rock has always been important in the lives of God's people. Water flowed from a rock in the desert to rescue the Israelites perishing of thirst (Exodus 17:6). Young David slew Goliath with a single stone (1 Samuel 17:50). Old Testament law called for adulterers, idolaters, and blasphemers to be stoned. Early one morning three women worried about who would roll a stone away from the mouth of a burial cave outside Jerusalem's city walls (Mark 16:3). Jewish unbelievers picked up stones and hurled them at the faithful Stephen (Acts 7:58). And the martyr remained calm as he looked into heaven and saw Jesus, the rock of his salvation.

Today Hasidim, or orthodox Jews, come to Jerusalem to pray at a granite wall known as the Wailing Wall. Mourners memorialize their departed loved ones by leaving white pebbles at grave sites. Construction codes require all public buildings in Jerusalem to be faced in granite. And rocks are always handy when the hatred between Jews and Palestinians turns violent.

Rock makes a good foundation for any building. Ancient ruins testify to the value of using stone for this purpose. The Wailing Wall in Jerusalem is a vivid example. So many centuries after its construction, so many wars later, so many storms and difficulties later, the granite wall is still there. We are building Christian homes that require a solid foundation—one that will endure through all of life's storms. Since you have chosen the Lord as your contractor, your Christian home can have such a solid foundation.

SLIDING TOWARD INSTABILITY

Are you concerned that the building you are in might collapse? It's unlikely. We take the foundations of our buildings for granted.

For a long time now, we have also taken for granted the foundation provided by the family. It once was the bedrock of our society—reliable, steady, supportive. But that assumption doesn't always hold true for our generation. The family today is fluid—a shifting, unsettled, and unsettling gathering of young and old. New laws, new technology, and new moral and ethical standards reshape our definition of family almost daily. As a result, the influence of family is questioned and under fire. Where family once almost universally implied stability, today it no longer enjoys that distinction.

Many people admit their family life is not very satisfying. They long for unity, peace, and harmony at home. They want more time with one another to cement relationships. They wish their families could be more caring and compassionate. They find something much different when they enter the doors of their own homes.

Many recognize unchecked self-centeredness and self-indulgence lurking about just beneath the thin veneer of respectability, eating away at the essence of family. Some search aimlessly for a sense of family purpose. Others have forgotten how families are supposed to function. Regrettably, they have no idea of what to do about it.

Christian families are under stress too. Some Christian families lack spiritual leadership. Parents feel incompetent or inadequate for studying Scripture together with their children. Husbands and wives have trouble sharing their faith with each other. They are driven by social values instead of gospel-inspired values. They are confronted by the media with false values or no values at all. Everyone else seems to believe that truth is what the latest poll says rather than what God says in his Word. Is it any wonder that even Christians sometimes question God's truth? Some Christian households teeter on the verge of spiritual dysfunction and disintegration.

All contemporary households echo the "hurriedness" theme. Most parents will tell you theirs is the *hurried home,* even before the term is defined. Some actually enjoy the pressure of feeling hurried. Others see it as a curse they are unable to address. In either case, the stresses of contemporary living are multiplied exponentially by the unrelenting change in the home environment.

American families, no matter what their cultural background, have undergone tremendous change in the last century. The changes have been dramatic, deep-seated, and widespread. Many children will not finish their formal schooling with the same mother or father figures with which they began. Most households no longer eat meals together. Meaningful communication is rare. Family conversations are often exercises in minimalism. We don't work well together. We don't like one another's company. We have little in common. And we don't really understand one another very well.

The changes have deeply affected the way we value things. Long-standing, traditional family roles and relationships are under attack. (We will have more to say about these traditional roles and relationships in chapter 6.) What's more, the rate of change, both from within the home and from without, seems to be accelerating.

Think, for example, of a family portrait taken one hundred years ago. Roles and relationships are very apparent in such a photograph. Father is clearly in charge. He stands at the center, or remains seated in the middle, his wife and children stand in silent witness to his leadership. How different that picture is from today's family!

Over the last century, the changes in and around the American family have been dramatic, deep-seated, and widespread.

In many respects the father-centered home of a century ago was more in agreement with the Bible's model. Scripture places the burden of responsibility for family leadership on husbands and fathers. Yet many self-interested men of a century ago exploited their status. In many states, for example, a husband was considered the owner of all marital property, including his wife's jewelry and clothing. Some states legally permitted a man to beat his wife, as long as it did not result in permanent, physical harm.

By the middle of our century, the family model had undergone significant change. Two world wars saw husbands and fathers fighting in remote regions of the globe. Their absence left a leadership vacuum at home. Women filled the gap. Mom was not only taking care of things in the workplace, she was also in charge at home. There were exceptions, but many husbands and fathers returned home to find their American home had become mother-centered.

In the '70s and '80s, family leadership was again up for grabs. The pill, feminism, new economic opportunities, and the advent of day care brought moms out of the home into the workplace. The media dubbed it "Women's Lib." This time no one rushed to fill the home's vacant center. Father was off doing *his thing*, as were Mom and the kids. In the "me decade," everyone was doing his or her own thing. The members of a typical family resembled ships passing in the night.

In many of today's homes, the center remains unoccupied. The family has never really recovered. The delayed impact of four generations of change is simply more than even a stable institution like the family can handle. Should we be so surprised that the fabric of the family is coming apart at the seams? Like the family of the man who failed to build a fire in the hearth, we have each become his or her own person. Family members remain disconnected and are not accountable *for* anyone or *to* anyone in particular.

As we approach the next century, diversity dominates the home scene. Some families are father-centered. But they seem like relics from the past instead of a wave of the future. The number of mother-centered homes still grows, proportionate to the ever-growing number of single moms. Some parents insist on permitting their homes to become child-centered. Clearly, this is not a God-pleasing model. And, sadly, a lot of families still have no real center. This cannot be God-pleasing either.

The social and cultural environments in which the family exists have also seen tremendous change. Our world knows the silicon chip, genetic engineering, lunar landings, interplanetary probes, the fall of communism in the Soviet Union, and lifelong education. *We communicate globally in cyberspace via a modem linked to the Internet.* How much of the preceding sentence would many of us have comprehended even a decade ago?

Have these changes affected families? How could they not? Today's college graduates can expect to change occupations—not jobs, but occupations—five to seven times in their lifetime. If that prediction holds true, that too will most certainly affect the family. No wonder we identify with the hurried home! The dizzying pace of our lives seems way beyond our control.

Or is it? Hurriedness, and the tension it brings into our lives, runs deeper than we may think. Some of that stress is beyond our control. But how we react and relate to these changes isn't. The adrenaline rush is as much a soul matter as it is psychological or physiological. In too many ways, many families are hurried because we build our homes on clay foundations. We have bowed to a pantheon of secret, false gods, carved from the soil of materialism. Were we living in Old Testament times, we could be put on trial for idolatry, a stoning offense.

If we really want to regain control of our hurried lives, we need to address our *wanting*. Hurriedness is a direct result of wanting more of something—more money, more rungs on a corporate ladder, more sex, more friends, more influence, more health, more stuff, more warm fuzzies, more trophies, more toys, more credit, more time. And more often than not, Christians follow along like lemmings.

We need to stop and consider the temptations and sin connected with our wanting. Wanting can so easily lead to discontent. At the heart of every hurried household lurks a sense of discontent—a driving need to feed our wanting. This is a spiritual matter. This underlying feeling that we never have enough is a dominant theme of our age—an abject fact we need to come to grips with.

Christian families caught up in the hurried lifestyle need to address the root cause of their hurriedness. But that will require resources none of us come by naturally. This is a battle for our souls. This battle calls for spiritual resources. It demands faith. The battlefield is our lives. And the war being waged has far more to do with our faith life and faith resources than anything else.

ROCK OF AGES

Masada is an ancient Roman fortress built atop a high desert plateau. Herod the Great, governor of Judea in Jesus' time, designed it as a refuge. Shortly after the Romans destroyed Jerusalem, Jewish zealots made a heroic last stand at Masada. Today Masada is a symbol of Jewish independence. The men and women of the Israeli armed forces take their loyalty oath there. Almost all pilgrims to the Holy Land visit Masada sooner or later. We did too.

Hannah, our Jewish guide, indicated that this was a very special place for her. She led us to the ruins of an ancient synagogue. As a young archeology student, she had excavated this very site. Beneath the granite slabs of the synagogue's floor, Hannah's team had unearthed an ancient manuscript—a portion of the Book of Ezekiel. Jews, she explained, believe that the Old Testament Scripture is a living entity. When a manuscript was worn out from use, they buried it as though it were the body of a dear relative.

Then Hannah began to read to us that portion of Scripture that she and her colleagues had discovered. It was Ezekiel's familiar vision of the Valley of Dry Bones. As she read, tears filled her eyes:

The LORD . . . set me in the middle of a valley;
it was full of bones. Then he said to me, "Prophesy to
these bones. . . . 'This is what the Sovereign LORD
says to these bones: I will make breath enter you,
and you will come to life. Come from the four winds,
O breath, and breathe into these slain, that they may
live.'" . . . They came to life and stood up on their
feet—a vast army. . . . "These bones are the whole
house of Israel" (Ezekiel 37:1,4,5,9-11).

We were moved. Hannah's reading made us reflect on the coming of Jesus and the life God has breathed into our sinful hearts. But this was Hannah's moment. And she was going to use it to make a confession of her Jewish faith. To Hannah the text meant something very different. The miracle of the valley of dry bones, she explained, pointed directly to the 1948 United Nations declaration that created the sovereign state of Israel. Hannah's faith rested in the Jewish hope for an independent national homeland.

Down through the centuries, people have put their faith in many things: money, intellectual acuity, their own abilities, military might, science and technology, political power, philosophies, commerce, and . . . the list goes on and on. Faith gives hope. Without it we give up. Every thinking individual, believer or unbeliever, has faith in something or someone, even if they do not call it faith. None of the things we place so much confidence in, however, can honestly promise to be one hundred percent fail-safe. Eventually, everything in which we put our trust will fail us. Everything, that is, but one.

The Bible defines faith as *"being sure of what we hope for and certain of what we do not see"* (Hebrews 11:1). Give that definition a little time to sink in. It explains why faith is so important when standing up to the forces that assault our families.

Nothing in this life is as *sure* or as *certain* as Jesus. Even family has never been able to fulfill all our hopes and dreams. But all the promises God gave us in Jesus are absolutely true. Jesus and all he brings to us is sure and certain no matter how uncertain the times.

Those who put their faith in Jesus will someday fully realize that dream in heaven's eternal family. We claim the love of God by faith in Jesus, and by faith we make all God gives our own.

> **Nothing in this life is as *sure* or as *certain* as Jesus. Even family has never been able to fulfill all our hopes and dreams.**

With the spiritual resource of faith, we grasp God's undeserved forgiveness and love. Martin Luther thought of this resource as a precious gift—one of the three pillars of the Reformation. *Scripture* and God's *grace* are the other two. The reformer taught that God's Spirit gives us faith even though we've done nothing to deserve it. Faith is not a mystical essence. You cannot see, touch, hear, smell, or taste faith because it is spiritual, not physical. Nevertheless, your faith is as real as your conviction that the earth is round.

Faith clings to truth. A strong conviction can stand up to even the most extreme challenges in the hope that truth will prevail. For Christians, when everything else dissolves into chaos, Jesus remains the pillar of our strength.

Today families struggle with truth. Knowing *whom* to believe and *what* to believe is a major concern. In some ways we are quite different from all the generations that came before us. We are, for example, bombarded with the kind of truth proclaimed by the media. There's the *truth* of so-called experts, the *truth* of celebrity, and the *truth* of good feelings. Many of us have become quite cynical about these claims. Sound bites and photo bites can have a powerful impact on what we believe, but we have learned to be cautious. Words and pictures can also be used to manipulate and deceive us.

Then there is the truth of scientific fact. Our world is always ready to listen to this kind of truth. But we can be deceived by science too. Sometimes theory is passed on as fact. And, in the end, the promise of science and technology is still unable to resolve mankind's moral dilemma. That is, we cannot invent our way to heaven and rebuild our shattered relationship with the Creator.

Ultimately all of science's claims cannot prevent death. Humans may live longer than they did a generation ago, but they still die.

The assault on the truth is sometimes quite subtle. That is because the assault comes from the father of lies himself, Satan. He loves to push our cynicism to the point of believing that all truth is relative. Like Pilate, we are ready to ask, *"What is truth?"* (John 18:38). That is a dangerous position for a Christian. A Christian's faith is based on divine absolutes: heaven and hell absolutely exist. God demands absolute obedience from his creatures. No sinful human can give God what he demands. But Jesus has provided the absolute obedience for all and has suffered once for the sins of all humanity. Those truths have stood for centuries and will stand for all eternity (Hebrews 13:8).

In our age the secular world debunks the idea of absolute truth. Our children have to contend daily with the notion that truth is only a matter of personal perception. It sounds philosophical, but this is quickly becoming the prevailing way of thinking. And it is effectively promoted at a level that every child can understand. Christian parents need to keep an ear to the ground and their eyes wide open. We need to understand the dangers that threaten faith if we are going to be able to defend ourselves and our children from them. But this bears repeating: Our fight will only succeed if we remain well-grounded in our Christian faith. Our faith must be strong.

In a generation that is obsessed with wanting more, Christians will want more of this powerful spiritual resource: faith. We should be asking: How do we get faith? How do we keep faith? And how do we get more of it? . . . for ourselves and for the other members of our families? The answer to all three of these questions is one and the same: faith in Jesus springs to life and grows whenever we hear God's Word.

Because the Bible exists in a world that deals only in relative and changing truths, it is an island of absolute truth for anyone in search of a sure and certain foundation.

The Bible is God's Word. What it tells us about ourselves and about God is absolutely true, down to the last detail. God never lies. Because the Bible exists in a world that deals only in relative and changing truths, it is an island of absolute truth for anyone in search of a sure and certain foundation.

The central absolute truth of Scripture is that Jesus is mankind's Savior from the terrible curse of sin. He is the only way to heaven, the only truth worthy of our complete confidence, and the only person to look to for a meaningful life. He is truly the only hope for our soul's salvation. Jesus has claimed all that for himself. He said, *"I am the way and the truth and the life. No one comes to the Father except through me"* (John 14:6).

God has revealed his loving plan for us in the Bible. When Christians speak about family foundations, they are speaking about reading and hearing and studying God's faith-building Word. Jesus is the bedrock that Christian families need to build upon. Faith in Jesus comes as God works within us through the good news of the Bible's truth. Christian fathers, mothers, and children must always remember that faith springs to life and grows whenever we hear Jesus' Word.

CONSTRUCTION MODELS

Scripture provides some wonderful, real-life examples of how faith interacts with God's enduring promises. One account details the life of a man named Abraham. You have already met Abraham's grandson Jacob in chapter 1. Abraham's name gives us a clue as to why this model of faith has important implications for us. *Abraham* means "father of many." Beyond his role as an ancestor of the Hebrew nation, this man of God is the father of all believers. In a spiritual sense, you and I are among Abraham's descendants. We are related to him not by blood but by faith. That's what the apostle Paul wrote: *"He [Abraham] is the father of all who believe"* (Romans 4:11).

Abraham's faith rested in God's promises. When God promised to give him a new land, like an obedient son, Abraham packed up his family and belongings and moved. He didn't know where he was going to live. He only knew that he trusted the Lord to act on his promise. The Lord never disappointed Abraham. He never changed his mind. He never lied to Abraham. Their relationship depended entirely upon God's faithfulness. Abraham simply trusted his God to keep every word of his sacred promise.

On one occasion God put Abraham's faith to the severest of tests. The Lord commanded that Abraham prove his commitment by sacrificing the life of his only son, Isaac. Supported by his confidence in the Lord's faithfulness, Abraham obediently traveled to the place God directed and marched up the mountainside with his son. He had every intention of carrying out God's command. Painful as it was to think about taking the life of his only legitimate heir, Abraham believed that God would find a way to restore Isaac's life. He trusted God so completely that he believed God would even raise Isaac from the dead if necessary. You see, earlier God had promised that the Messiah would come through Abraham's son Isaac. Abraham was absolutely convinced that God would not go back on his promise, no matter what happened on the mountain.

God's faithfulness did not disappoint Abraham. God spared Isaac's life and provided a substitute sacrifice—a ram ensnared in a nearby thicket. God's sacred promise was secure and intact. Abraham's title as "Father of Many" was still viable. God's own faithfulness had found a way to make it so.

We believe because of God's powerful energy in our hearts imparted through the gospel. But there are other models of God's construction. Remember Peter? Peter's name hints at this man's tremendous faith. Petra was an impenetrable rock fortress in the southern part of Palestine. It guarded a heavily traveled mountain pass, which served as a trade route from the east to the west. Jesus gave Simon the name Peter because of his rocklike faith. But Peter, "the rock," crumbled under pressure. It happened on the night of Jesus' trial—a night when Peter's faith was at low ebb. In the face of danger, Peter denied three times that he even knew Jesus. On that shameful night, Peter was hardly rock-solid.

> **Peter's faith was not focused on his own strength of character or ability; it was founded on the things that Jesus had taught him.**

And that wasn't the first time something like that had happened to Peter. Perhaps only a year earlier, impetuous Peter tried to walk on water. His heart was in the right place. He wanted to be like Jesus. After a few steps on the water, his faith withered, and he sank. Jesus had to come to Peter's rescue and remind him to put his trust only in God.

But this same man was also capable of extraordinary expressions of faith. When the Lord asked Peter and the other disciples who they thought Jesus was, impetuous Peter replied, *"You are the Christ, the Son of the living God"* (Matthew 16:16). Peter's simple confession pinpointed the object of his faith. It was Jesus. At that moment Peter's faith was not focused on his own strength of character or ability; it was founded on the things that Jesus had taught him. That's when Jesus gave him the name Peter.

Peter's confession of faith rested in the same reassuring promises that Abraham trusted. He put into words what already existed in his heart of faith. And his *confession* became the heart-beat of faith for many generations of believers to come. This is the bedrock we want our homes to stand upon: faith in God's sure promises, faith like that of Abraham and Peter. God's Spirit has planted the seed of that faith within us. In faith we are able to cling with superhuman tenacity to the Lord's enduring promises. In faith we have confidence that Jesus will never fail us.

CORNERSTONE AND CAPSTONE

An architect uses points and lines to design buildings. On paper a building's foundation and its walls all relate to a single point. During construction that point is fixed with a marker at one corner of the foundation. The *cornerstone* is laid to mark the exact location where two walls will eventually be joined. The building's entire alignment depends upon the precision of the cornerstone.

Churches, schools, and other public buildings often have the date of construction carved into the cornerstone. Thus the cornerstone also fixes the building's position in time and history.

A second critical stone in construction completes the walls. This stone is referred to as a *capstone*. In the ancient world, the walls that protected a city from invaders were finished when the capstone was put in place. When the stone workers set the capstone on a building, the project was as good as finished.

Jesus is both the cornerstone and capstone of our faith. He is both the founder of our faith and the finisher of our faith. He keeps us true to himself as he extends us in many directions. And he keeps us steadfast to the very end. One great old hymn (coincidentally penned by Samuel Stone) declares, "The Church's one foundation is Jesus Christ, her Lord; She is his new creation by water and the Word. . . ." How true! We couldn't build on a firmer foundation than Jesus. His life and death line up perfectly with his Father's holy will. And through Baptism we too are perfectly aligned with our heavenly Father's will.

Jesus is both the cornerstone and capstone of our faith.

Jesus pointed to himself when he quoted Psalm 118:22, *"The stone the builders rejected has become the capstone"* (Matthew 21:42). He was—and still is—that stone. He came to finish what he had started before time began. On Calvary's cross he declared it for all people for all time in a final triumphant gasp: *"It is finished"* (John 19:30). The plan to save mankind from sin's curse was complete.

Our kinship with Jesus was sealed in Baptism. With the gift of faith, which he gives us, we can claim our rightful place in God's household. In faith we were adopted into his Father's holy family. In faith Jesus our Savior is also Jesus our brother, and we are brothers and sisters with one another. No other cornerstone could be truer. No other capstone could ever make our salvation more complete and more certain.

Nor will we be treated as orphans in God's holy family. We are his treasured children—adopted from eternity for membership into his household at the price of his holy, precious blood. He has made us full-fledged heirs of heaven's majesty and glory. Without Jesus, certain peril and death await us. With Jesus our safety, security, and life are guaranteed. One old hymn proclaims, "On Christ, the solid rock, I stand; all other ground is sinking sand."

Faith and the Word of God are tied together.

We stand on the solid foundation of Jesus by faith. The Scriptures remind us that faith comes when we hear the gospel, the good news of Jesus. Paul reminded the Romans, *"Consequently, faith comes from hearing the message"* (Romans 10:17). That's not an isolated thought in Scripture. Faith and the Word of God are tied together. Paul wrote to the Ephesians, *"You also were included in Christ when you heard the word of truth"* (Ephesians 1:13). Jesus taught the connection between faith and his Word with an illustration. Two builders constructed new homes—one on rock, the other on sand. When a furious rainstorm raged against both houses, only one house was left standing—the house built on rock (Matthew 7:24-29).

Jesus explained that hearing his Word and putting it into practice gave the house that stood the strength it needed. The gospel writer adds that the crowds who heard Jesus teach this truth were amazed at his authority. They should not have been so amazed; it was none other than the author and finisher of faith who taught it.

A HOUSE OF LIVING STONES

The word picture of rock reappears often in Scripture. Considering the Holy Land's geography, that's to be expected. Stone is one natural resource that will never be in short supply in this part of the world. Rock is everywhere. Anyone who has ever lived in this land understands rock's agricultural impact, its significance for travel and commerce, and its influence on architecture.

Rock is a natural Bible metaphor for another reason: we associate the quality of absolute lifelessness with rock, which helps teach divine truth. Jesus referred to the lifeless stones when the Pharisees complained about the praise of the crowd on Palm Sunday. Jesus said, *"If they keep quiet, the stones will cry out"* (Luke 19:40). Certainly everyone knew the stones could not talk, but such a miracle was not too great for his power on such a dramatic occasion.

Ezekiel, the Old Testament prophet, recorded another beautiful rock word picture. The prophet described how Jehovah brings his people to faith: *"I will give them [my people] an undivided heart and put a new spirit in them; I will remove from them their heart of stone and give them a heart of flesh. Then they will follow my decrees and be careful to keep my laws. They will be my people, and I will be their God"* (Ezekiel 11:19,20). These words are pure gospel. They illustrate Luther's point that faith is a gift. Like stone we "cannot by [our] own thinking or choosing believe in Jesus Christ . . . But the Holy Spirit has called [us] by the gospel" (Luther's Small Catechism: The Third Article of the Apostles' Creed). It's a spiritual miracle, a radical surgery that God performs within our souls. Hearts of lifeless stone—as ours once were—have been transformed by faith into living stones.

In and of itself, that message is astounding, unexpected, remarkable. But it is still only part of the story. There's more!

Faith is a personal matter. Each one of us believes. Our eternal future depends upon the faith we hold within our own hearts. Faith is not a thing we can split and share like a loaf of bread. We cannot give faith away or let someone else borrow our faith for a little while so that they can get into heaven. You have your faith and others either have their own faith or they have none. But we can share Jesus, and we should tell others about what we believe, especially those we love the most in this world—our families.

As personal as faith is, God doesn't want us to enjoy our gift alone. We are social creatures. Remember, he created us to be social creatures. Our faith has a wonderful social dimension. God gives us daily opportunities to express our faith within the community of other believers and beyond. As the Author of faith, he has commissioned us to be part of his eternal building project. He has hired us on as his workmen. And our job description is quite specific: to share the joy of our faith with the whole world.

This is all part of a divine building program—a feat of spiritual engineering genius! We, *"like living stones, are being built into a spiritual house"* (1 Peter 2:5). One by one the master engineer gathers us and shapes us with the precision of a divine craftsman. Then he fits us together into a living temple, dedicated to the glory of our Savior. As he uses us to build, we continue to work—urgently sharing what we believe with others. He pours his divine resources endlessly into the project. As we tell others about our Savior, God works through that witness to do again and again the miracle Ezekiel speaks of. We proclaim his saving gospel in a thousand different ways. And as we do, he blesses each new phase of construction.

Construction goes on 24 hours a day. Nothing stands in its way. Jesus is himself the chief architect, the builder, the foundation, the cornerstone, and the capstone. He has done it all, and he has done it well.

Construction goes on wherever God's Word rules in living hearts that now beat with faith in Jesus. The building goes on every time we confess our faith in him. Law and gospel are the tools. We bring our infants to Jesus in Baptism. We teach God's saving truth to young and old.

God's Spirit always uses Word and sacraments to bring us to faith and strengthen us. But the story of how we individually come to faith and remain in faith is unique to each of us. Our individual stories need to be shared. Families need to celebrate them, cherish them, and retell them over and over.

Some Christian families have difficulty sharing their faith with one another. The reason most often given for despising God's Word is that they don't have enough time. But let's not hide behind excuses. Some complain that they don't know enough to share their faith. We can find more excuses than we need if we really want them. But the Lord has made us living stones so that we can support other living stones who also believe. He has also asked us to be part of his building project. We are to share the gospel. And as we share God's good news, the Holy Spirit makes unbelievers—spiritually dead rock—into new living stones.

Some members of the early church at Rome seemed reluctant to share their faith with others. Perhaps their newness to the faith inhibited them. Many of them were gentile pagans converted to Christianity. They lacked the background for understanding the Old Testament. Some of them probably were shallow and weak, spiritually immature. The apostle Paul might have excused them from working on God's construction crew. But Paul refused to do that. His admonition was gentle, but compelling: *"I myself am convinced, my brothers, that you yourselves are full of goodness, complete in knowledge and competent to instruct one another"* (Romans 15:14).

The *competency* Paul was referring to was not founded in their own intellectual powers or in their own inherent goodness. They were *good* because Jesus' perfection covered their imperfection. Their *knowledge* was not a reference to a high IQ or a graduate degree in philosophy or theology. They had the knowledge of faith. They *knew* Jesus and the salvation he came to bring them. They possessed the two essential resources necessary to get on with the program—forgiveness and knowledge. Their job was to build. Paul was telling them to use their resources and get the work done.

You have those same resources. In the privacy of your own home or on the job, at the health club, or on a playground, you are competent to instruct others. You have what it takes. You have Jesus' own goodness . . . and you know Jesus in your heart of faith! You can instruct those who are nearest and dearest to you. You are competent. You are *good* in God's eyes because Jesus is good. You have the *knowledge* you need by virtue of your faith. You have the right stuff to do the most important job you will ever have. Go. Do it.

BUILDING OBJECTIVES:

- To ground the faith of your family in God's Word.

- To develop habits that will put you in daily contact with his promises.

- To learn to distinguish the difference between law and gospel. God reveals himself to us in these two essential Bible teachings.

- To encourage the members of your family to be active in their church membership. You each have a place and a purpose in the fellowship of God's people.

BUILDING BLOCKS

- Set aside ten minutes together as a family to read the Bible. The time can be after mealtime, before bed, or before everyone goes off to the day's activity. Begin by reading a gospel like Luke. Leave your Bible where you can see it, and read a chapter or a section a day.

- When you come home from church, discuss what each member of the family learned from the worship service.

- Review the difference between law and gospel by using the catechism your children use for confirmation instruction. Look in the question and answer section that deals with these two main teachings of the Bible.

- Ask your older children to explain what they believe to the younger ones. Sometimes the younger children will surprise you by their faith and confession. Give them an opportunity to say what they believe too.

4. FRAMEWORK

Families invariably experience stress. The raging storms of life will test faith to its limit. Sooner or later they will threaten your home too. When the foundation of your home is rock-solid, the house can withstand the assault. Still, the most vulnerable part of your home rises above the foundation. Choosing the right lumber to frame out your new home is vital.

In good times, and especially in bad, love is the stuff that holds families together (Ephesians 4:2-5). It cements relationships and binds up wounds. Even unbelievers talk about love when they describe the successful family.

The Christian's understanding of love is connected to the love we have experienced in Jesus. In faith we know the price God paid to make us his. His sacrifice demonstrates real, unconditional love. His building materials were two rough beams of timber and a handful of nails. The builder, of course, is the carpenter's son. His cross is our tree of life. His story tells us of his great love for us. From it we learn there are no limits or boundaries to his love.

The rare timber used to construct the frame of your spiritual home comes from Calvary. As we contemplate the great love of

God for us, we learn what love is. We sense a pattern for our own love of others. The more we work with God's love for us, the clearer is our discovery of two powerful truths: The first is that the big timber of God's love is strong enough to help you withstand the worst of life's storms. The second is that God will use all those storms for your good.

THE AMATEUR CARPENTER

Temporarily, you'll need to halt construction, step back, and do some hard thinking. You need to wrestle with an important question: Why did God give you a family?

The question assumes you consider your family to be a gift. People whose lives have been tortured by family conflicts find it hard to think of their family in this way. If you are among them, the question is vitally important. Perhaps you need to step back even farther and pause even longer with this question: Just why did God give you a family?

You may never have considered this question before. Take your time. You may want to pause briefly and write a few thoughts on paper.

There are, of course, a lot of right answers. Perhaps you have considered one of these: God gave us families as a way of bringing children into his world, or God gave us families to have people to love, or God gave us families to have someone to take care of, or God gave us families so we could pass Christian values along to a future generation. All fine answers.

One answer is better than all the others. It goes something like this: the one significant reason God gave us each a family is that Christian families help point one another heavenward. In this answer heaven is our ultimate goal. Any other reasons God may have had for giving us families are all secondary. This is not idle speculation; Scripture leads us to this conclusion.

Family is yet another powerful dimension in God's desire to bring all humans to eternal life in heaven. He gave us family so we could care about one another and nurture one another in his Word. He gave us family to listen to one another for understanding and to admonish one another when sin threatens faith. Yours is a Christian home so that you can keep one another focused on your heavenly objective.

Many of us have not always done that as faithfully as we could. A few of us have missed the point completely. Some of us have passed up precious opportunities to nurture the other members of our families with God's Word. We haven't called attention to sin when it was our loving duty to do so. We've failed to provide examples of Christlike behavior in our own lives. At times we have been reticent in regard to maintaining a regular pattern of worship and prayer life at home. In short, we've failed very often!

> **God gives us families so we can encourage one another on our way to heaven.**

Perhaps we found excuses. We reason that as long as we keep food on the table and spend time in the company of our spouse and kids, we've done our duty. That was the mistake made by the man who built a new home for his family, but forgot to build a fire in the fireplace. Many of us are guilty of squandering God's precious gift of family by neglecting their spiritual needs.

These are, for the most part, sins of omission. But that doesn't make them any less deadly. They were as costly for Jesus on Calvary as murder or rape. And, of course, we are forgiven. But that's never an excuse to continue in our failures. We have many opportunities to do better. We are new creatures; Jesus is our new master. We live for him now. And he gives us the power to live a life that pleases God. Our lives change.

Real love comes from God. It is impossible to know love in the fullest sense without knowing God's forgiveness. We understand his love best when we know the terrible price he paid to redeem us. That sacrifice is what makes his love more valuable than any other treasure. Without it we could never hope to have a share of heaven. Christian families have a wonderful added benefit. Because they know how God loved them, they know what love is all about, and they have a pattern for their relationships with each other.

LOVE AND PAIN

But for many people, God's love raises a troubling question. They reason that if God is both good and loving, he could not or would not permit his people to endure sorrow or sadness.

Suffering can assault faith in a powerful way. When a family is stricken with heartache of any kind, an ominous question rises to the surface like a monster at sea: If God really loves us, how could he let this happen? When you find yourselves asking this question, the storms of life are beating against your home at hurricane force. Your faith is severely battered.

For a moment let's consider an event in the lives of our Lord's disciples (Mark 4:35-41). A deadly storm whipped the Sea of Galilee into a froth around the disciples' tiny fishing boat. They feared for their lives. This probably wasn't a time to wax philosophical, but for the sake of discussion, let's imagine each disciple asking *the* question: If God really loves me, as he says he does, how could he allow this deadly squall to threaten my life?

Again, for the sake of discussion, we might imagine that their answers would vary. One disciple might have been inclined to see the predicament as a case of incredibly bad luck. Another might have concluded that Satan was setting another of his wily traps. Maybe one of them was a naturalist. His explanation for the deadly storm would have been that this was just nature's random way of recycling everything in due time. Their thoughts were probably not so clearly articulated, but they surely had to be asking why. Why was this happening to them? Perhaps one of these men had to be wondering if he was being punished for some terrible sin. Another perhaps thought that he didn't really deserve to suffer such an untimely fate.

In Psalm 107 a poet wrote about storms in another way: *"They saw the works of the LORD, his wonderful deeds in the deep. For he spoke and stirred up a tempest that lifted high the waves"* (verses 24,25). Perhaps the disciples knew this psalm from memory. But James, John, and the others would surely have taken exception to the psalmist's choice of words. With the wind threatening to capsize them and the waves pouring over the gunwales of their tiny boat, God's deeds hardly seemed "wonderful."

Should they have believed something else? Perhaps that the Lord created the lovely winds and the beautiful waves to be admired by nature lovers, while some other ungodly force made the terrifying, deadly aspects of nature. That's not a very comforting thought. It means that God is only in control of some things, some of the time. And that is just not true. Jesus proved he is in control of all things when, moments later, he commanded the winds to cease and the waves to be calmed and they obeyed.

Even if the disciples had recognized that their peril was something sent by God, it would have been difficult at that moment to see it as a gift. Hindsight would have been the only perspective from which to see the wind and waves as blessings.

So it is. When life is at its stormiest, it is especially tough remembering that God created the wind and the waves and controls all things. It's difficult to recall then that his plans for us were laid out in eternity, according to his own good purpose. When one is suffering, it is difficult to understand how this could be God's will. At times like this, we won't agree with the direction in which the Lord is taking us, especially if it involves pain or sorrow.

Nobody wants to drown at sea in a sinking boat. But in faith we can learn to accept whatever God's direction might be, knowing that it will always be for our good. Sometimes—usually later—we are even able to see these hardships as gifts to be appreciated and cherished. The disciples learned a valuable lesson during that stormy night! Later they would certainly have recognized the storm as a gift. They talked about it, and the lesson was so important the Holy Spirit caused it to be written down for us. But hindsight so often provides perfect vision. Perhaps in time, and certainly in eternity, hindsight will be our best perspective too.

But God has his own good reasons for permitting these tempests in our lives. Like the disciples we confront our own limitations. In times of hardship and trouble, we lose the illusion that we are in control. At those times we recognize how helpless we are. That's a painful and unsettling realization. Yet God challenges us at those times to turn to him for help. The disciples did; their example is our guide. When we turn to Jesus for help, he strengthens our faith. He promises to work in our hearts through the comfort we find in the Scriptures. The Scriptures assure us again and again that God does indeed love us, no matter how severe the storm or sharp the pain. Remember Abraham. His faith depended upon God's faithfulness. Because the Lord Jehovah proved over and over that he could be trusted, Abraham believed.

The Scriptures assure us again and again that God does indeed love us, no matter how severe the storm or sharp the pain.

Saint Paul knew adversity in his lifetime. He survived a hurricane and shipwreck. He experienced persecutions, insults, and other hardships. And he struggled with a personal source of pain that Scripture never described in detail. He had his "thorn in the flesh." About that struggle Paul wrote: *"Three times I pleaded with the Lord to take it* [this torturous ailment] *away from me. But he said to me, 'My grace is sufficient for you, for my power is made perfect in weakness'"* (2 Corinthians 12:8,9). So Paul too came to see his limitations. In the next verses in 2 Corinthians, Paul wrote that his own weaknesses clearly demonstrated the greater power of Christ.

Job knew suffering too. He knew it was good for him. He hated every minute of the pain he had to endure, but it kept him humble. It reminded him that he and his Creator were not equals; God was God, and he was but a mortal. Job's suffering led him to realize that God could do anything he wanted with Job's life. This helped Job see the bigger picture and the good God was doing for him through his suffering.

Jesus gave us another reason to see our trials in life as blessings. He invites, *"Come to me, all you who are weary and burdened, and I will give you rest"* (Matthew 11:28). God's love shines so brilliantly in that promise of the Savior! He draws us ever closer to himself through those raging hurricanes of life. In Jesus, and in Jesus alone, we find comfort, rest, and strength.

God has yet another reason for sending us storms in life. It is the reason most closely associated with his purpose for giving you a family. When life's storms threaten others, we are presented opportunities to share God's love with them. In these opportunities God gives purpose and meaning to our lives. We serve him by comforting and encouraging the people near to us and dear to us, especially when they are hurting or in trouble. *"We are God's workmanship, created in Christ Jesus to do good works, which God prepared in advance for us to do"* (Ephesians 2:10).

Disappointment, frustration, pain, trial, and misery will come to you and the members of your family. Perhaps they have already made an unwelcome entrance into your family life. Families don't need pat little answers to pain. They need love and compassion. Christian families know Jesus and the power of his faithful love. In pain and difficulty, individual members of each family have clear opportunities to show the concern and compassion of Christian love to those who hurt—to the child, to the parent, to the teen, to the grandparent, and then to those outside the family circle too.

LOAD-BEARING CROSSBEAMS

How do we learn to be compassionate human beings? In which of the elementary grades is mercy taught? Is there some kind of training that teaches us how to care about others? What curriculum embraces a concept like burden-bearing? Can we develop godly attitudes about justice or kindness on our own, or do they need to be taught?

We live in a troubled world. It doesn't take a rocket scientist to see that our society is being stripped of its moral fiber. As our values degenerate, our heart for one another wears thin. Self-centeredness and a lack of compassion go hand in hand. Much of the erosion can be traced to the spiritually dysfunctional home. The reason? Compassion is taught best and first in the context of family. And today too many families have simply failed to nurture the idea of caring about others.

Picture the Christian cross. Consider its simple construction. If the vertical timber of your relationship with your heavenly Father is secure—and it is because God has done everything to make it secure—then you are ready to set the horizontal beam into position. That's picture talk for suggesting that it's time now to think about our human relationships within the home.

The approach to this step in construction is straightforward. Jesus himself etched the instructions onto the blueprint in blood with the words *"Love each other as I have loved you"* (John 15:12). His love is the vertical beam; our love for others is the horizontal. His life, death, and resurrection bind the two together. As the hymn writer so beautifully put it:

> See, from his head, his hands, his feet,
> Sorrow and love flow mingled down.
> Did e'er such love and sorrow meet
> Or thorns compose so rich a crown?
>
> Were the whole realm of nature mine,
> That were a tribute far too small;
> Love so amazing, so divine,
> Demands my soul, my life, my all.

Grace is breathtaking, isn't it! So astoundingly beautiful, so stunning that it's hard to know how to react. His love deserves some kind of a response, but what? Nothing we do or say could ever begin to repay him. But the Christian asks anyway, "How can I make my life count more for the One who gave his life for me?"

The tribute we bring is our humble service to others. We serve him by building others up in faith. And we build one another up in faith using the same gospel tools God used to build us: patience, kindness, humility, goodness, honesty, hope, perseverance. Others see God's love when they watch us in action. Love is an action, remember?

The New Testament proposes a whole collection of love actions for anyone who would follow Jesus:

- Be devoted to one another (Romans 12:10).
- Honor one another (Romans 12:10).
- Accept one another (Romans 15:7).
- Speak to one another (Ephesians 5:19).
- Submit to one another (Ephesians 5:21).
- Bear with each other (Colossians 3:13).
- Teach and admonish one another (Colossians 3:16).
- Encourage one another (Hebrews 3:13).
- Spur one another on (Hebrews 10:24).
- Greet one another (1 Peter 5:14).

Your Christian faith is a way of life. It weaves its way through the warp and fiber of ordinary days, among ordinary people living ordinary lives. The Savior's love lives in you. He turns your life into a real-life drama about concern and compassion for others. And you have the leading role.

> **Your Christian faith is a way of life. It weaves its way through the warp and fiber of ordinary days, among ordinary people living ordinary lives.**

Sometimes your compassion will bring you into direct conflict with sin. Admonishing a fellow sinner is never easy. When you are called upon to admonish, you will need to remember, in all humility, that you too are a sinner. Admonish with compassion.

Sometimes you'll be dealing with the mayhem that sin leaves in its wake. You stop to offer a cup of cold water because someone is thirsty. It's what Jesus would have done. You offer a word of encouragement—a kind word, a smile of love, a touch of compassion.

You wait patiently, vigilantly, and soon the parade of opportunities marches by. You will be amazed at just how many opportunities there are. Sometimes the sheer volume can even become a little overwhelming. What a glorious reason for living! What an honor God has given us! How meaningful life in a family can become when we reach out to one another with God's love. For when we do, we are helping one another remain focused on our heavenly goal.

Isaiah explained how it works by asking the rhetorical question:

"Is it not to share your food with the hungry and to
provide the poor wanderer with shelter—when you see
the naked, to clothe him, and not to turn away from
your own flesh and blood? Then your light will break
forth like the dawn, and your healing will quickly
appear; then your righteousness will go before you,
and the glory of the Lord will be your rear guard"
(Isaiah 58:7,8).

That's God's love, living in our actions. What a dynamic way to live a new life!

Someday Jesus will echo Isaiah's words. He will make a declaration of his own: You fed me when you fed others. You visited me in prison when you visited others. You clothed me when you clothed others. Your love in action is the proof of your faith. The circle is complete (see Matthew 25). When we care about others in the same way that Jesus has cared for us, we are living and giving for him.

RAFTERS, TRUSSES, PLANKS, AND SAWDUST

The compassionate life of a Christian carries a high price tag. The secular world usually responds to genuine love with ridicule and disdain. Unbelievers despise us for our godly intentions. And the burdens of others, that we shoulder for Jesus' sake, inevitably leave painful scars.

Nothing could leave deeper wounds in the life of a Christian family than one of its members living in jeopardy of eternal damnation. A child who refuses to remain under God's forgiveness brings unparalleled heartache to a Christian parent. A brother or sister dying in unbelief represents unmatched grief to the surviving members of a Christian household. A Christian would be willing to endure any pain, perhaps even death, to see a change of heart.

Sometimes a Christian home can resemble a battlefield. The conflict rages when a Christian's only recourse is to address sin with the convicting power of God's law. The law brings some people to their knees in repentance, but it hardens the hearts of others. Calling someone you love to repentance carries huge risks—necessary risks. Calling someone to repentance can be a full-blown hurricane.

Jesus once said that he did not come to bring peace, but a sword. He was referring to God's law. The way it penetrates human hearts is always painful. When a family member persists in rejecting the law's convicting message, that stubbornness can divide a home. The sin of unbelief pits *"a man against his father, a daughter against her mother, a daughter-in-law against her mother-in-law."* Jesus said, *"A man's enemies will be the members of his own household"* (Matthew 10:34-36).

Where sin threatens to overrun faith, our loving duty is to assume the risks. Spoken with humility and grace, our intervention can lead to repentance. It takes courage, but all of heaven will be watching and cheering when the law reaches its target.

But sometimes we need help. Both the Christian family and the church possess God's healing tools: law to burst the balloon of sinful pride and gospel to heal and make us whole again. Sin needs to be confronted. Grace needs to be pronounced. The church and the Christian family are both in a unique position to minister to anyone navigating in life's deadliest storms. The church and the home share the same gospel mandate to intervene. Both carry the responsibility and the risk for encouraging the weak. They work together reclaiming lost sheep, defending the fatherless, speaking up for those who have no voice, warning of sin, and declaring God's grace.

In recent decades Christians have been too willing to abdicate this role to others. We have been turning to the humanities more frequently for relief from family stresses. Psychology and sociology can be very beneficial in helping us understand our relationships with one another. God gives us those tools to be used with good judgment. But many family conflicts have spiritual problems at their root. So often the issues involve sin, forgiveness, and the healing power of God's love. Secular views on the human condition don't address sin from a spiritual perspective.

The home and the church need to reclaim this ministry to at-risk individuals and dysfunctional families. This is spiritual territory. A ministry of compassion is every Christian's turf. Caring for others is not an optional clause in a Christian's contract. We can do all the other things well. We can preach and teach to our heart's content, but if we have not love, we are nothing (see 1 Corinthians 13). Love is not just a word; it is an action, remember?

First generation Christians of the New Testament church set a precedent for us that still serves as a useful model. The daily distribution of food to widows and orphans was apparently beginning to become a problem. On one hand, the apostles had a responsibility to preach and teach God's Word. On the other hand, someone needed to be concerned for the welfare of these women and children. The Roman government did not pursue a national welfare policy in the way we do. The solution was to select seven men who would carry out this ministry of compassion on behalf of all of God's people. The church organized itself for this unique kind of ministry. The program eventually led to training and equipping people to carry out this special work. Perhaps we need to review that model and restudy the principles that drove it.

We learn to find our strength for sharing one another's burdens in the promises of our Lord Jesus. Even when the words of comfort and encouragement are not a natural part of our vocabulary, God's Holy Spirit provides the words we need. When we remember that it is God's love, not ours, working in and through us, compassionate living is a deeply satisfying way to journey through life. It promises rich rewards and blessings aplenty.

We can do all the other things well. We can preach and teach to our heart's content, but if we have not love, we are nothing.

BUILDING OBJECTIVES:

- To look for opportunities to help others.
- To listen to others with love and concern.
- To pray for the needs of others.
- To develop a list of Bible texts that have been of special comfort to you under stressful circumstances. And use them to provide comfort, hope, and encouragement to others.

BUILDING BLOCKS

- Read 1 Corinthians 13 together. Let each member of the family confess a personal failure to live according to the model of love. After each confession encourage one another to love better. Make the encouragement specific and concrete rather than general and vague.
- Let every member of the family share a Bible passage that has helped them. Relate the circumstances when the Bible passage was especially helpful.
- Pray for one another. Take the troubles, concerns, and joys of another family member to the Lord in prayer. Give each member of the family an opportunity to pray out loud for another member of the family.
- Do one thing for someone else each day. Some examples: say a kind word, help with a chore, allow someone else to choose, help a brother or sister get ready for school.

5. THE COMPLETE
LIGHTING PACKAGE

Your new home is making wonderful progress. Your architect, the Lord, has been with you day and night. Your well is deep—a never-ending flow of God's grace. Your home's foundation is rock-solid—immovable and unchanging—secured in Christ's own Word. And the structure has been framed out with the costly lumber of the cross. God has truly blessed your project. You knew he would. Now it's time to give some thought to your home's interior. The lighting, in particular, calls for your attention.

We tend to take lighting for granted. But poor planning could result in dim shadows and dark, forbidding corners. The wise builder combines natural light with reflected light to bathe the living area in a joyful and inviting ambiance.

Light from the sun warms the earth. It makes it possible for us to see where we are going—to be mobile. Life would be impossible without light. Plants couldn't grow, the food chain would not exist, and there would be no warmth.

Light also exposes things, as in photographic exposures, radiation exposure, or exposure to a bright, new idea. Criminals prefer to operate in the dark, where illegal activities cannot be detected.

When their deeds are exposed in the light of the truth, the courts can prosecute them.

Light dispels darkness; the converse is not true. The instant you open the door between a lighted room and a dark room, light from the lighted room floods into the dark room; but darkness from the dark room does not even seem to affect the lighted room. As Alice in Wonderland would say, "How curious!"

NOTHING LIKE THE BEAUTY OF NATURAL LIGHT!

Light is the first thing God created in his universe. Moses' account in Genesis hints at the uniqueness of this divine invention: *"In the beginning . . . God said, 'Let there be light,' and there was light. God saw that the light was good, and he separated the light from the darkness. God called the light 'day,' and the darkness he called 'night.' And there was evening, and there was morning—the first day"* (Genesis 1:1,3-5). Notice the intimate connection between light and time. These verses tell us about the origins of both. Notice also that from this moment on, every mountain, every ocean, every living organism, every planet and star, everything done at the Creator's hand would be bathed in light for all to see.

The apostle John picked up on these first words of Scripture. In beginning his own gospel, John deepened our understanding of God's light by adding this inspired dimension:

> *In the beginning was the Word, and the Word was*
> *with God, and the Word was God. He was with God*
> *in the beginning. Through him all things were made;*
> *without him nothing was made that has been made.*
> *In him was life, and that life was the light of men.*
> *The light shines in the darkness, but the darkness has*
> *not understood it* (John 1:1-5).

John was speaking about the coming of God's Son into the world. Life, light, and God's powerful, creative Word all packaged in one person—the Son of God and Son of Man, Christ Jesus. *"The Word became flesh and made his dwelling among us."* Then John added, *"We have seen his glory, the glory of the One and Only, who came from the Father, full of grace and truth"* (John 1:14).

Some kind of light! John saw it. The disciples witnessed it in person. And, with the eyes of faith, you and I have seen his glory light shining even into the darkest places of our lives. God sent his Son to illuminate a world steeped in the hopeless darkness of sin. All of his light is good, like that light created in the beginning. It is good because his light is filled with absolute truth and divine grace.

The New Testament era began with a spectacular light show on the slopes of a little-known village named Bethlehem in Judea. It terrified local shepherds.

Thirty-some years later, the same Jesus, born on that holy night in Bethlehem, took three of his followers—Peter, James, and John—to the top of a mountain. There they saw something that no other earthbound human being has ever seen—a glimpse of the glorified Christ. And they reported to the world, *"His face shone like the sun, and his clothes became as white as the light"* (Matthew 17:2) Luke adds the comment, *"His clothes became as bright as a flash of lightning"* (Luke 9:29). It must have been an unforgettable sight.

God's light is indeed something to be desired in our own hearts and homes. His light is good because it comes from him. We will want to walk in his light during our lifetime on earth. And we can look forward to basking in the glory of his holy light for all of eternity. What blessings God has for his faithful!

Sometime during the 40 years of wandering in the desert, the Lord instructed the priests of Israel to bless the people in a special way. They were to say, *"The LORD bless you and keep you; the LORD make his face shine upon you and be gracious to you; the LORD turn his face toward you and give you peace"* (Numbers 6:24-26). Ever since, God's people have been repeating the words of that profound blessing. It is a beautiful, comprehensive blessing that captures the essence of everything we desire most. One day we hope to stand in his glorious heavenly presence. Now we desperately desire the peace that only his love can provide. We long to have our heavenly Father look at us, face-to-face, and be pleased with us, as a father is pleased with his children.

But can you imagine standing face-to-face with God! His face is so gloriously bright with holy perfection that it consumes anything unholy. That's a scary thought for creatures of the rebellion. We exclaim with the psalmist, *"Who can stand before you when you are angry?"* (Psalm 76:7). Who of us would be so foolish as to risk exposure to the Lord's radiant face? Who would want God to show his face in their home?

The answer might surprise you: We would! Protected by Christ's own perfect life, his obedient death, and his victorious resurrection, living in his radiant light is not only possible, it is a reality. Because of Jesus we are forgiven, declared holy, and called saints. Light, his light, the light of life, is ours, free for the taking. All we need do is bask it in. And that is precisely what God wants us to do.

The mighty Word, which brought time and the universe into being, floods the pages of Scripture with divine light to point us in the direction of Jesus. He is the Light of the world—past, present, and future. The family that remains steadfastly connected with God's Word has already seen his holy light; it glows warmly in their hearts. The Lord's face has already turned in our direction. And it has not consumed us. Does that sound like your household? John was talking about you when he wrote, *"We have seen his glory!"* (John 1:14).

> **The family that remains steadfastly connected with God's Word has already seen his holy light; it glows warmly in their hearts.**

But about the time we realize how special divine light really is, a bottom-line kind of question intrudes: *Why would God do all this for us?* Why did he create our world and place us in it? Why did he show us mercy when we deserved none of it? Why did he dispatch his Son to this planet of wicked people to live and die on their behalf? Why did he plant the seed of faith in our hearts? Why did he cause thousands of years of history to be recorded in Scripture for our edification? Why does he extend to us the hope of living in eternal bliss with himself? Why would God go to so much trouble? *Why?*

The answer is as plain as day. God is love! We can see it on the gentle hillsides of Bethlehem where, for one moment in history, a supernatural light illuminated the darkness in a way that has not been duplicated before or after.

That night a light split the black Judean sky with such majesty that the gospel writer could only describe it as *"the glory of the Lord"* (Luke 2:9). An angel appeared, hovering between heaven and earth. The shepherds, trembling in utter terror, needed to hear, "Don't be afraid." Then the angel proclaimed an astounding message. It was good news—personal news—news that set the heart of each one of those shepherds aglow. Yet it was news that would bring much joy to all who heard it: the Savior, Emanuel, the Messiah promised long ago, had been born in their village. They were told to go and find him, see him, touch him, worship him. The angel told the shepherds exactly how they would know that the baby they found was the One they were seeking.

Then, before the shepherds could catch their breath, the angel was joined by countless ranks of heavenly beings. The night sky was ablaze with glory. The song they sang echoed in every direction, and the music, though not the least bit unfamiliar, was heaven's own. The host of heaven sang, *"Glory to God in the highest, and on earth peace to men on whom his favor rests"* (Luke 2:14).

The Judean hills look the same today. For three days our sleek, new double-decked touring bus wove its way through the Judean hills, taking us to places of special interest. Each day we begged our driver to pull over so that we could get off the bus to photograph the Bedouin shepherds that made the route so picturesque.

On our last day, our driver gave in. Perhaps a dozen of us got off and began clicking away. But within minutes the native children hurried in our direction. With outstretched hands they begged, "Dollah! Dollah!" as they ran. As they came closer, we were repulsed. They had not bathed or had their clothing washed for quite awhile. The little ones coughed a terrible croup, mucous ran from their noses, and some had crusty, red scabs from scalp lice. They reached for our cameras and grabbed at our pockets. We had all we could do to wrestle our way back onto the bus.

When I regained my composure, I suddenly realized it was to people just like those children that God had first announced the birth of his Son. I had found these people despicable and disgusting. God had not. He loved them. And he, the holy, mighty God of Creation, was even willing to be born into their world, to live and die for them. And that shamed me and my attitude. That tiny baby in the Bethlehem manger brought glory to his Father's name, where we could not. He came to earth in complete humility. He came to serve the needs of sinners. And that alone would bring glory to his Father.

But the good news doesn't end there. We have a share in eternal glory as well. Jesus wants us to experience the glory of his holy presence in heaven. He promises to reward us with a place before his glorious throne. Our voices will join with the heavenly chorus, glorifying the name of our Savior-God forever. God's own glory light will be the only light we will ever need or want. His glory light will sustain us for eternity. Sin and evil will no longer threaten us. Divine glory will forever replace earthly suffering. And we too will shine like the sun, basking in the eternal glow of God's holiness.

Do we deserve it? Not in the least. His glory can only be our glory because of his mercy and grace. He deserves all the credit. He deserves all of the glory. He deserves it, and he refuses to share his glory with pretenders.

THE FAMILY ALTAR

As Abraham moved from place to place, the Scriptures tell us he built altars. He built one at Shechem when he first arrived in the land God had promised him (Genesis 12:7). Then he built one east of Bethel (Genesis 12:8). After spending time in Egypt, Abraham returned to that altar. He moved his tents again and built an altar near the great trees of Mamre at Hebron, near the place where he eventually buried his wife Sarah (Genesis 13:18 and 23:19). In his day there were no churches, synagogues, or tabernacles. Abraham's altars served as places of worship.

We aren't told much about Abraham's activity at those altars, but they were, no doubt, places where Abraham spent time considering his relationship with the Lord. He probably offered sacrifices there. It's likely he said prayers and recalled from memory the stories of God's love that had not yet been recorded in written form. Perhaps he recited the Lord's sacred covenant promise. Each time Abraham visited one of those altars, he was expressing his gratitude for the Lord's many blessings.

In one description of Abraham's worship, we are told that Abraham *"called on the name of the LORD"* (Genesis 13:4). This phrase suggests that Abraham's worship involved other people. His voice could be heard. In other words, Abraham's faith was a matter of public record. Such a proclamation of God's promises among other people is called *confession.* Since Abraham had a large household, we might naturally conclude that he shared his faith with the members of his household. The home, it seems, is a natural setting for sharing faith at a very intimate level.

Christian families can also build altars in their homelife. For some the idea of a family altar might even be taken quite literally, that is, an actual place where they worship the Lord. Perhaps worship is even at a specific time every day so that it becomes a family ritual or routine. Family members look for ways to come together daily to worship God. They select a pattern that can provide opportunities to confess their faith to one another. As Christians we confess our faith with our mouths (Romans 10:10). We articulate the power of God's saving truth in our lives. The key is to establish a regular, daily habit that involves as many family members as possible. The family altar invites full participation from moms, dads, grandmas, grandpas, visitors, and especially children.

The kind of activity that takes place at the family altar will vary. It includes prayers at bedtime, at mealtime, or at the beginning of a new day. It involves family members in discussions and devotional activities, readings, or singing hymns and spiritual songs. In homes where there are young children, the family altar provides time for teaching Bible stories and becoming familiar with Bible characters. Teens need time to talk about issues. They are searching for solutions to a growing list of life's challenges. Christian homes provide plenty of opportunities to help them search in the light of God's Word.

When there is a crisis, Christian families come together to pray. They turn to God's Word to find strength and comfort. Many of the psalms work especially well in the family setting. And special days such as birthdays, anniversaries, baptisms, weddings, births, and even deaths become reasons to celebrate God's goodness and grace or to turn to his Word for strength and comfort.

The devotional family dedicates time and energy to worshiping God. Its members set aside time daily to think about God, talk about his love, study his Word, worship him, and pray to him. Like the flow of God's abundant blessings, our expressions of love and gratitude are never-ending. When we know that we are receiving God's gifts anew each day, we have good reason to stop whatever we are doing in our busy lives and say thank you to God.

Home worship is different from typical church worship. But the elements are still the same: We come together. We hear God speak to us in his Word. We acknowledge his goodness. Then we send one another out into the world as salt and light. But the interaction at home is more intimate. Home worship mingles the generations in a unique way. It brings together the wonder and excitement of childhood, the idealism of youth, the realism of middle age, and the wisdom of old age.

Home worship mingles the generations in a unique way. It brings together the wonder and excitement of childhood, the idealism of youth, the realism of middle age, and the wisdom of old age.

Home worship sometimes needs to be highly structured and well organized. But the home setting also has many moments when spontaneous dialogue occurs. These are difficult to find in church. At home everyone can participate at his or her own level of understanding. At home individuals can shine in their worship life. Unique gifts and talents can be offered as part of a living sacrifice to God. Concerns, perspectives, and insights can be shared. And at home, even children can make personal confessions of their faith. There they can feel freer to "call upon the name of the Lord" in a safe forum. And they can begin to practice sharing their faith and formulating their personal confessions.

We are, as God created us to be, social creatures. We connect with one another. We interact. We communicate. We confess our guilt to one another—another kind of confession. And we are especially eager to share the intimate knowings of our faith with one another. Our confessions help us encourage and correct one another. They help us sharpen our understanding of the gospel message. They help us define our teachings and distance ourselves from those who would distort God's truth.

We are social creatures. We connect with one another. We interact. We communicate. And, as Christians, we are eager to share our faith with one another.

At the family altar, God's Word is never an afterthought. Used as God intended, the Bible is the most practical book ever written. The apostle Paul listed four simple ways to use Scripture: *"for teaching, rebuking, correcting and training in righteousness"* (2 Timothy 3:16,17). Virtually every aspect of family life is covered in that short list.

God doesn't expect parents to be theologians. But he does give us the important responsibility of nurturing family members. We become more confident in doing that through daily practice. And, as our confidence grows, we become more willing to take risks, bringing an openness and honesty to family discussions. Here even the most private and personal concerns can be shared in the light of Jesus' Word.

Children see things in ways most adults no longer can. Kids understand their world through an active imagination. In response to a teacher who asked her class how Jesus got into their hearts, a four-year-old piped up, "He just walked in on my tongue and slid right down." Not bad. Few adults could do better at explaining how we come to faith.

Christian mothers and fathers need to see imagination as a wide-open door of opportunity for teaching Bible truth. Kids think in pictures. Adults tend to intellectualize. We analyze, synthesize, and construct models to try to make sense out of things. If we are not careful, we can also intellectualize Bible truth.

The imagery God used to reveal himself to us in Scripture is rich and diverse. Yet it is simple and profoundly meaningful: a dwelling place, an innocent lamb, a farmer, light, the fragrance of incense, a vine, bread, a stream of water, a bride and a bridegroom, the wind, a king, a father, a judge, a stairway to heaven, and many more. These pictures of God's power and grace cannot be easily erased from the mind's eye. We can use our imaginations to see Jesus walking on water, restoring the dead to life, healing lepers, casting out demons. And there are snapshots of us and our con-temporaries there too: burning flax, salt, clay pots, stonework, lost lambs, wandering sheep, whitewashed burial caves, and wheat fields. Relationships in every word picture. Bible truth brought to life as we put ourselves onto God's divine film.

God's Word is always simple truth. But it always challenges us to grow in our understanding. We need to seek spiritual maturity without letting the truth becoming cluttered with too much adult thinking. When you read the Bible together . . .

- think of it as having one purpose and one point of focus. The point of focus is Jesus. The purpose is to strengthen our faith in him.

- learn to accept the things God tells you with the simple faith of a child. Some parts of the Bible will stretch the limits of human reason. And some things in God's Word are simply beyond our human understanding.

- thank God for his Word. It is an extraordinary gift. And give everyone an opportunity to express his or her appreciation for its blessings.

- become familiar with all of God's Word. The truths spoken of in one part of the Bible are supported in other places.

- don't let someone else's intellectual level of understanding become an obstacle to your appreciation for Scripture. And don't look for hidden messages or secret codes. God does not speak to his people in double-talk. The Bible is meant for people of all intellectual levels of understanding, including the very young, uneducated folks, and even those who have trouble learning and remembering things.

- don't try to make the Bible say things you want it to say. Don't ignore or avoid some of the Bible's teachings either just because you don't like them. All of the Bible's truth belongs to God. We are free to discuss it, even systematize it; but God does not permit us to tamper with or distort its meaning. The Bible's message is timeless; it does not need to be updated or rewritten to meet contemporary concerns or issues. Its truth will always be relevant to mankind's dilemma. On the other hand, Scripture needs to communicate clearly. Accurate, new translations are helpful because they can help people understand God's truth even better.

- ask for help when you don't understand what Scripture is saying or when you are faced with what seems to be a contradiction. Don't hesitate to use topical indices, concordances, chain references, commentaries, and study guides. But if none of these resources satisfies your questions, ask someone who has more Bible background.

- note key Bible texts that you cling to as personal favorites. Write them down. If possible, memorize some of them. Then you can refer to them quickly when you are faced with situations in which you need them.

- finally, don't allow anything to sabotage the regular, daily pattern of spiritual activity in your home. Review your reasons for devoting time and energy to worshiping God and hearing him speak to you daily in his Word. The devotional home is the result of a conscious, sanctified choice. Ask God to provide the strength and will to become a family devoted to seeking his will.

DECISIONS! DECISIONS!

Worship is a choice, a conscious decision. There was nothing accidental or unintentional about erecting a stone altar out in the middle of the desert, as Abraham did so many times. Going to church is an act of the will; but so is staying in bed on Sunday morning. Spending five minutes together at home to study God's Word every night after supper is a choice; but so is dashing off helter-skelter, too busy to even recite a prayer of thanks together as a family. None of us is so driven by circumstances that we have lost control over the daily worship choices we make. We owe it to God and to ourselves to at least be honest about that.

God doesn't want pretend glory, nor does he want our devotion if it is merely a response to his law. There wouldn't be anything genuine or sincere about praise forced by the demands of the law. God wants us to honor his name by our own sanctified choice. Before we belonged to his family of believers, that was impossible. But, in the brilliant light of Jesus—covered in his radiant goodness—our lives are able to reflect his glory in everything we do and say.

Worship finally amounts to anything a Christian says or does in Jesus' name—every choice rendered, every decision made. Each new decision is yet another opportunity to give glory to God—a confession of our faith to anyone within earshot. Looking to buy a new car? Somewhere in the decision-making process is an opportunity to praise your Savior with some godly thinking. Planning to have children? Another worship choice. Deciding on your future occupation in life—college, tech school, military service? God's name will be glorified in the way you go about making that important choice. You will be sending a message to anyone paying attention to your life-choices. They reflect Jesus' light. You are a citizen of a brilliant and beautiful "city set on a hill" (see Matthew 5:14-16). The world cannot ignore you, even though it may hate you.

Decisions. Decisions. Every one another opportunity to proclaim the name of him who rules in our hearts.

That is exciting news for every Christian household. A Christian family has opportunities to make one statement after another about Jesus to a world dying in sin. The opportunities are so abundant and pass through our lives with such blinding speed that we could never hope to seize every one. They are simple, everyday choices— the stuff of life. For example: the films and books we choose for entertainment, the way we handle our money and possessions, the language we use and the tone of our voices, our attitudes about sex, our contributions of time and energy to the community, our business dealings and the way we treat other people. Decisions. Decisions. Every one another opportunity to proclaim the name of him who rules in our hearts—to reflect his glory, his love, his forgiveness to a world that gropes about in spiritual night. The light we reflect to others is the light that dispels all the dark hopelessness in their lives. That's what "walking in his light" means. *"You are the light of the world. A city on a hill cannot be hidden"* (Matthew 5:14). That's a mission statement for us if ever there was one!

BUILDING OBJECTIVES:

- To desire God's light for your household and seek it in his Word.
- To take time and devote energy to worshiping God together with the other members of your family every day.
- To look upon every decision as an opportunity to serve God and seize as many of these opportunities as possible.

BUILDING BLOCKS

- Read Psalm 121. Let every family member express what the promises of the psalm mean to him or her.
- Read Genesis 12:1-7. Discuss your family altar with your family. Where is it? What should happen there? What can you do to make your family altar a better place or time to glorify Jesus?
- Read Matthew 5:13-16. Discuss how members of your family can let their light shine before men.
- If you have had difficulty establishing a regular routine for family devotions, consider reading sections of a gospel for 30 days. Matthew can easily be divided into 30 sections.

6. THE OPEN HEARTH

The homes we build must be places where families will want to come to be together. They should invite conversations that are important and meaningful. In the sanctity of the Christian home, we will laugh together, work together, cry together, worship together, and pray together. So build your spiritual home with relationships in mind. Without them your house will be empty and cold.

Two sad figures kept company on the path that led from Jerusalem to the little village of Emmaus. Their Lord had been crucified a few days earlier, his body hastily laid in the darkness of an unused tomb. Their lives had been woven together with his; his message had filled them with such hope and joy. On that journey to Emmaus, their future seemed fragile at best. They talked about the emptiness they felt inside, and they wondered about the future.

A stranger joined them. He talked; they listened. Only later did they realize they had spent a few hours with the risen Lord Jesus. But when this fact finally dawned on them, their perspective on life changed dramatically: *"Were not our hearts burning within us*

while he talked with us on the road and opened the Scriptures to us?"
(Luke 24:32).

If only our homes could be places where hearts burned
within! Then they would be vital places, filled with the dynamic
energy all families need.

They can be. Our households can be full of hope, unity, and
peace. God has made us his and sustains our faith through the
wonderful news of his love. We can have a measure of heaven on
this side of eternity, home fires crackling with the healing warmth
of the Savior's voice. With the promise of heaven firmly in our
grasp, life on earth can have new meaning. And we can experience
a joy that the unbelieving world will never know.

A PLACE FOR EVERYTHING
AND EVERYTHING IN ITS PLACE

The last thing God created was a family. No infusion of the
breath of life. Not even a divine word of creative power. Not that
the Almighty could not have done it that way. But human relationships are a special gift—a gift God wanted human beings to witness. So the Lord carefully orchestrated its unwrapping.

First, God put Adam in charge of the garden. Immediately
Adam's life had a newfound sense of purpose and meaning. But
Adam also needed to learn a very important truth. So God arranged
for Adam to do a survey of all living things. In this way, Adam
began to see that his life was incomplete.

The parade of living things that Adam recorded in his memory was
impressive. But none of the world's living creatures was like him. Fish
and birds were unable to admire the earth's vast beauty and engage in
a lingering conversation. The trees and grasses didn't provide the
human affection Adam desired. The animals didn't look forward, as he
did, to the walks and talks with the Lord. So Adam longed for someone
like himself—someone to share his love for the Creator and his appreciation for the Lord's handiwork. This was not a character flaw; Adam's
yearning was good, and it thoroughly accomplished God's purpose.

The survey taught Adam much about himself. It led him to realize he needed another creature like himself—a counterpart with whom to share life's adventurous journey. There was God, the almighty Creator of all Adam saw. But Adam certainly was not his Creator's equal. So it was important to find someone like himself—an equal. Adam needed someone who was intellectually, physically, emotionally, and spiritually like him. As God had said, *"a helper suitable to him"* (Genesis 2:18). In short, the survey taught Adam what it meant to be a social creature. It showed him that he was missing something . . . or *someone.* What a curiously wonderful notion: *needing another someone* to complete our lives.

Social interdependence was part of God's plan from the beginning. In this, the first human relationship, Adam and Eve complemented each other down to the last detail. In a human relationship, they could truly be all that God intended. And in this unique relationship, like all of God's creation, they would bring glory and honor to the Creator.

When Moses was inspired to record this history of our first parents, he understood that this was God's way of establishing family: *"For this reason a man will leave his father and mother and be united to his wife, and they will become one flesh"* (Genesis 2:24). The circumstances made this a remarkable statement. Neither Adam nor Eve was born to earthly parents. Nevertheless, Moses held their union up as a model for all time. A new family begins when a man and a woman separate from their parents and commit themselves to each other. This lifelong union is blessed in a miraculous way. Two incomplete, independent individuals join to become a whole unit. They embrace each other in a physical, emotional, intellectual, and spiritual compact—a marriage.

This was the first link in a great genetic chain that stretches from Adam and Eve down to your family and mine. It represents the past, present, and future of the human race. The first family was constructed according to God's ideal. Sin had not yet entered the world. The relationship between the first husband and wife was in perfect harmony with God's eternal will.

> **The five God-given family roles spoken of in Scripture—husband, wife, father, mother, children—provide stability and order for the Christian home.**

Even after the Fall, the marriage relationship, as well as other family roles, provided a structure for living in harmony with God's will. This structure provided for social order as well. The Bible outlines distinctive, God-given roles for husbands and wives. Martin Luther identified five family roles from Scripture: husband, wife, father, mother, and child. God instructs husbands, for example, to love their wives in the same self-sacrificing way that Christ demonstrated on Calvary (Ephesians 5:25-27). Wives, at the same time, are to relate to their husbands in the same way that the church submits to the Lord Jesus, who is the head of the church (Ephesians 5:22-24). Both are driven by a selfless love for the other.

When marriage partners observe these roles, a husband and wife complement each other in a God-pleasing way. When husbands and wives refuse to function according to their God-given roles, they run the risk of destroying their marriage.

When a marriage is blessed with children, new roles and relationships emerge. The biblical model (Ephesians 6:1-4) indicates that Christian fathers and mothers are to give their attention to nurturing their children. They have the responsibility especially to teach their children about Jesus. In his wonderful structure, God placed children under the authority of their parents. Childhood is a time to learn obedience to God-ordained authority. Parents, on the other hand, are warned not to overstep the limits of their authority. To do so only frustrates the nurturing process.

The collapse of the family is related, in part, to our stubborn failure to function according to these godly roles. Husbands are reluctant to lead. Wives are unwilling to follow. Children are taught by the media to rise up in rebellion against parents, who are portrayed as foolish and inept. Parents are all too willing to turn the nurturing of their children over to others. The economic stresses of contemporary living and the lifestyle we've adopted conspire to make professional child care an appealing alternative. Sometimes we are even willing to share our nurturing responsibilities with people who do not profess faith in Jesus. This is a serious matter, having implications for the souls of the next generation.

THIS ROOM'S AMBIANCE

A floor plan puts rooms to practical uses. At least it should. Victorian mansions, for example, almost always included a parlor, a library, and a sitting room. In the Victorian era, they were practical rooms.

Courting took place in the parlor. And when there was a death in the family, the body was laid out in this room to give mourners a chance to pay their last respects. The library was the home's center for aesthetic and academic development. Music lessons, painting, letter writing, and study were usually restricted to this room. Sitting rooms were usually smaller. Intimate conversations took place here.

The floor plan for our spiritual homes should highlight the importance of family communication. Relationships are shaped by the way in which we talk with one another and listen to one another. The offices of family therapy counselors are crammed with sad examples of poor family communication. Too many people have simply never learned how to talk with the other members of their family. This is probably as true of Christian households as it is of unbelievers' homes.

God takes an interest in the way in which his people communicate. He understands communication. He created us to be social creatures. He gave us the gift of language. He speaks to us in words of truth, and he listens to us when we speak to him in prayer. God's interest in every single member of your family stretches to the cross of Jesus. Each member of your family is a redeemed child of God. The love of God for us all gives every Christian home an advantage. The communication that occurs within the four walls of a Christian home is—or ought to be—under the influence and direction of the great architect.

The communication that occurs within the four walls of a Christian home is—or ought to be—under the influence and direction of the great architect.

What the members of your household say and how they say it will encourage, support, comfort, and build your home or it will discourage, frustrate, tear down, and destroy your home. That is not an exaggeration. The importance of honest, direct, and loving communication can never be overstated. In the Christian home, such communication sets the stage for sharing the one thing that can bring joy, peace, and unity to your family—the gospel. Failure to communicate will frustrate the very gospel that brings so many blessings. The principles of godly communication apply to every social setting and all human relationships. But they especially apply to life in the Christian home.

Most of us understand the rules for speaking, even if we don't always apply them. They address attitudes of the heart. And they are amazingly simple. God gives us these principles:

- Be honest (Ephesians 4:25). But temper your honesty with love (1 Corinthians 13).
- Encourage one another (1 Thessalonians 5:11).
- Don't find fault with others (Matthew 7:1-5).
- Keep your tongue under control (James 1:26).
- Don't punctuate your conversation with swearing (Matthew 5:37).
- Build others up instead of tearing them down (Romans 15:1,2).
- Talk about things of lasting value—things worth treasuring (Philippians 4:8).

A Christian's entire life, not just speech and conversation, is governed by two additional principles—love and forgiveness. We are to love one another deeply (1 Peter 1:22), and we are to forgive one another (Colossians 3:13). We are reminded to forgive others every time we pray the Lord's Prayer. Christians don't just harbor these principles in their hearts; they express them in action and words. They speak of the love and forgiveness that is in their hearts.

If the words that come out of our mouths affect the health and stability of our homes, so does the time we take to listen to one another. But the rules for healthy listening are not always well understood. Good communication is a balance of speaking and listening. Secular communication experts encourage us to listen to one another to demonstrate respect for and acceptance of others. But a Christian's act of listening is more than a token of good will. It is far from passive. For Christians the main point of listening is to learn what another person needs:

> Tell me your story.
> What happened?
> Tell me how you feel about that.
> Does it anger you?
> Are you hurting?
> What do you believe in your heart of hearts?
> Do you know that you have sinned?
> Do you know that you are forgiven?

The purpose of listening goes far beyond idle talk. We who know God's love in our own lives have something vital to offer others. We listen so that we can determine whether it's the right time to talk about God's expectations or the right time to share his love and forgiveness.

Sometimes the conversation tells us that we need to bring the full force of God's law in touch with a heart that is stubbornly unrepentant. Sometimes our listening reveals an opportunity to forgive and guide the heart of another so that *next time* he or she will respond according to God's will. Wise Christian parents never dwell on bad behavior, even though they have to call attention to it. They forgive as Christ forgave, and then they look for ways to stress *next time* to their children.

Careful listening can also uncover pain, fear, loneliness, confusion, or an overwhelming sense of guilt. Unchecked, these emotions will lead a Christian to despair. Satan would love that. Despair makes us give up on God's promises; it sabotages faith. Any hint of despair is a call for comfort. The look of fear or loneliness is a plea to once again hear of God's abiding presence. Confusion and indecision need to be addressed with words of divine comfort and guidance. Talk of guilt is an urgent call for reminders of the forgiveness that was won for us by the blood of the Lamb.

Satan uses the things we say to plant the seeds of mistrust, envy, and hatred in our homes.

The key to good communication is always in the listening. We pray for a discerning heart—one that shows compassion with patient listening. Then, when it is time to speak, the words we choose will be effective and appropriate.

Satan uses the things we say to plant the seeds of mistrust, envy, and hatred in our homes. Our words can frustrate, infuriate, confuse, alienate, hurt, demean, deceive, manipulate, or they can comfort, encourage, calm, instruct, uplift, and enable. The devil has, in fact, inflicted a great number of casualties on us by attacking the communication patterns of our homes. Three strategies in his arsenal, in particular, have brought trouble again and again.

The first is to confuse family priorities. Satan's age-old ploy is to make us uncertain about what really is important. He tempts us to spend less time with one another. He gets us to believe that our relationships and responsibilities outside the home are more important than those within the family setting. The myth of "quality time" compounds our confusion. Some of us have bought into the idea that we can have family togetherness without actually being together.

Satan's second strategy is to wage an all-out assault on intergenerational relationships. What once was referred to as a "generation gap" has grown to be an abyss. In many homes young people, middle-agers, and seniors are simply unable to carry on a meaningful dialogue. Our rapidly changing technology, and the economy and culture connected to it, have given us the false impression that we have little in common. What a shameful tragedy! Subculture peer groups are slowly replacing family as our primary social structure. Even some churches prefer to address members in peer groups instead of family groups. We need to do a better job relating to people who are unlike us.

Third, the enemy of God and the family seeks to dismantle the family, relationship by relationship. Over the last century, his attacks on the husband-wife relationship have accomplished that many times over. It is a natural point of attack, since marriage between one man and one woman serves as the foundation to family living. Yet Satan has been having major success attacking yet another family relationship—one that is another quite logical point of attack—the relationship between fathers and sons.

The relationship between a father and a son is especially fragile. A young man bears the responsibility for separating from his childhood home to start a new family. In a sinful world, the motives for separation have the potential for being misunderstood. And such misunderstandings are bound to wreak emotional havoc. When a son pulls away from his parents to become independent, the process is particularly stressful on the father-son relationship. Fathers grow concerned when their adolescent sons begin making plans and decisions for themselves. Such independent thinking becomes confused with disobedience and rebellion. Often a son's decisions are not the decisions a father would make. Some fathers make matters worse by planning their sons' lives with goals and objectives too closely connected to their own lifelong dreams. A son's failure to share his father's dreams can be misinterpreted as rejection. Often that damaged relationship is never repaired.

Men and women are emotionally different. That is one reason they complement each other so well. Men suffer relational stresses in ways quite different from women. The male instinct is to drive painful emotions deep below the surface. The male battle cry is "Move on! Proceed as though nothing happened." And it works . . . for a while. As a result, a lot of men, including a lot of Christian men, hurt in stoic silence over unresolved conflicts with their fathers and others.

Quite often these painful emotions do not resurface until sons become fathers. Then those repressed emotions erupt and get acted out. Without intervention, the cycle is likely to repeat itself in one generation after another. Unaddressed, the rift between alienated fathers and sons can be violent and abusive. Christian households are not immune; and frequently faith suffers.

All three of Satan's strategic ventures against the family hinge on the way we carry out our God-given family roles. They gather a head of steam when our communication patterns fail to be selfless, patient, and loving. They are spiritual challenges because they threaten faith. They deserve our attention, our concern, our prayers and efforts.

Genuine joy, peace, and unity are rare these days. The world knows how to laugh, but only those who know God's mercy have the kind of joy that promises to have the last laugh. The Pax Americana has come, and some day it will go, but the Prince of peace has called us into his peace, to live in peace with one another. Our love for one another, exercised in the shadow of the cross, is what binds us together in perfect unity. In Christ Jesus we are one in faith, one in spirit, with one goal, living to please one Lord and Savior.

TALK WITH THE BUILDER

Construction work is difficult work. You could spend yourself to exhaustion wrestling with all the issues involved in building a spiritual home. Jacob is a good case in point. After he fled his childhood home to live at his uncle's place in Paddan Aram, Jacob's life seemed charmed (Genesis 29–32). He matured. He worked hard. And God blessed him with a large family and great wealth.

But Jacob's estrangement from his father, Isaac, and his brother, Esau, continued to haunt him. His plans always aimed for the day when he would return to the land of his father. He would one day have to face the sins of his past; he accepted that.

After 20 years with his uncle, hundreds of miles from his home, Jacob packed up everything he owned and quietly slipped away. He led his entourage in the direction of home.

Jacob anticipated the worst. He sent messengers ahead asking for his brother Esau's favor. But the messengers returned with the report that Esau was bearing down on his position with four hundred men. Jacob turned to the Lord in prayer, reminding the Lord of his gracious promise to make him prosper. As Jacob prepared for the meeting with his brother, he was filled with fear and apprehension. After prayer he settled on a strategy for the dreaded meeting with his brother. He divided his camp into two parties, hoping that at least one would escape. Then he sent wave after wave of gifts toward his brother as a peace offering.

On the eve of his anticipated clash with Esau, Jacob quietly moved his family and possessions across the Jabbok and placed himself between his oncoming brother and his family. Alone and vulnerable, Jacob suddenly found himself wrestling with a stranger. The wrestling match continued all night until the break of day. When the two wrestlers had fought to a standoff, the man touched Jacob's hip, wrenching it out of joint. The injury crippled Jacob for life. But it served as a constant reminder of that remarkable night.

Hobbled by a dislocated hip, Jacob persisted. The stranger was God himself. And Jacob boldly told the man he would not let him go until the man had given him a blessing. He held God to the promise he had made at Bethel 20 years earlier. God assured Jacob of his blessings by issuing him a new name, Israel. The name means "he struggles with God." One day Jacob's offspring would be known as the "children of Israel"—a nation of God's people, people who struggle with God.

We share Jacob's new name. Of every Christian it could be said he or she struggles with God. Whether we find ourselves turning to the Lord to lift us up when we have lost a job or calling out to him in the night because the pain is too great to bear, the Lord wants us to struggle with him. He wants us to hold him to his promises, and he has made some remarkable promises to his believers. Through our struggles with God, we are taught over and over the lesson that all our blessings come from him.

Our relationship with our heavenly Father is not a distant one. It is as intimate as a wrestling match. We give this wrestling with God a name; we call it prayer. In prayer we have the ultimate communication platform—intimate, personal, direct, immediate, and profoundly effective. And it is exclusively designed for our use. Only the members of God's household have access to this powerful tool.

Prayer is for our benefit. How easily we become confused about that! We foolishly think that our prayers are for God's benefit—that he needs our prayers in order to know what is going on in our lives. He doesn't. God knows what we need long before we ask, but he wants us to ask anyway. He wants us to know that our help always comes from him. He wants us to remember that it is impossible for us to live apart from him. Without prayer we Christians would remain cut off from the source of all our daily blessings. The wonder of prayer is that God responds. He listens, and he acts in response to our prayers.

Not counting the gift of salvation, prayer could well be the most practical of all the gifts God has ever given to his people. For those of us who spend our lives looking for action, prayer is the answer. It gets things done. It is a bold, robust lifestyle—a mindset, a choice. If you have been waiting patiently throughout the pages of this book, wondering what you can do to make your home a joyful place to live, here is another answer. This is where you can go to work. Prayer is something you can do to make things happen.

The Bible tells us, *"Nothing is impossible with God"* (Luke 1:37). That is a very powerful statement. It asserts an absolute. Think about how exclusive the word *nothing* is. Consider your own limitations. All the impossibilities for us are entirely possible for God. We are talking about a kind of power here that the human mind is not able to grasp. He is, as we have already noted, the Creator of all things. He is, as we have already seen, in control of all things— wind and waves, light and darkness. He rules with absolute authority and divine power. And, with prayer, all of it is made available to the members of his household.

But if prayer reflects God's power, it also reflects God's great love for his redeemed. We are living witnesses not only to God's boundless might but also to his unfathomable love. Our petitions to the throne of grace are stitched to the Father's sacrifice on Calvary's altar. Without Jesus there would be no approaching God's holy throne. In Jesus prayer is yet another expression of God's covenant promise that nothing will impede, interrupt, or intervene in our cherished relationship.

Prayer is a family affair. To describe it, Jesus pictured a father unable to refuse his children's requests.

Prayer is a family affair. When Jesus taught prayer, he pictured a father unable to refuse his children's requests. He simply loves them that much. Jesus said we could ask our heavenly Father for *anything.* He hears, and he answers the prayer. What an astounding promise! *Anything* is another one of those absolute words that remove any and all limitations. Assuming that the things we ask for are in keeping with God's holy will and are for our good and the good of other believers, the possibilities are infinite.

Jesus prayed. He prayed not just in Gethsemane but also often by himself, away from the crowds. And his prayers were more than merely examples for us. Jesus prayed because he desperately needed his Father's strength and comfort. He prayed because he was experiencing the kind of stresses in his life that we experience in ours. He was fully human; he needed prayer every bit as much as we do.

We need to see the practical value of prayer. In prayer we talk to the builder of our homes. It opens the doors of God's entire warehouse of resources for us. In a crisis we come together to pray for God's help. In times of celebration, we turn to God to offer our thanks in songs of praise. In moments of weakness, we call upon the Lord to provide strength. And we turn to his power whenever we stand in the face of temptation. When we are so tired we cannot think, we collapse in prayer, seeking his energy and renewal. In the dark hours, we search for his guiding light. In times of fear, we turn our concerns over to him, confident that he will act on our behalf and for our good. He can do nothing less. He is our Creator-Father. His love demands that he come to our rescue in each and every need.

How blessed we are! Since the Fall all of creation has been tormented by the powers of evil. Yet we are among the privileged few—children of the Father, wrestlers with God—through faith in Jesus. With the gift of prayer, we can overcome a whole host of devils. Redeemed in the blood of the Lamb, we have the confidence that he will answer every prayer. His promise is to give us exactly what we ask for . . . or something even better.

One final thought regarding prayer. A lot is made these days about prayer technique. That may be good. Most of these techniques demonstrate how easy it is under any circumstance to talk to God. Circle prayers and family prayer-sharing are great innovations for teaching spontaneity. But spontaneity should not become an end unto itself. All valid prayers come from hearts of faith in Jesus, whether they are spontaneous or not. Prayer is a fruit of faith. Neither a prayer's polished resonance nor its candid spontaneity is what brings it to the Father's attention. Faith is the only thing that counts. And that faith is grounded in God's grace and mercy. When we have faith in Jesus, God hears our prayers . . . and answers. We have his word on that.

Families who really want to stretch their prayer life can do three things to make it more exciting. The first is to pray more for others. This is a natural extension of the life of service that we dedicate to the Lord Jesus. The second is to pray not so much for a better life but for more faith to endure life's trials. And the third is to remember to say thank you to the Lord for all his daily blessings. It is too easy to forget that all things come from God, especially when things are not going so well. Even the wrestling is itself a genuine blessing, difficult as that can seem.

BUILDING OBJECTIVES:

- To honor the God-ordained roles for members of the Christian household: husband, wife, father, mother, child, submitting to one another in selfless love.

- To communicate with one another honestly, directly, and lovingly.

- To take the time to be an active listener, ready to address one anothers' spiritual needs.

- To pray—especially for a stronger faith. To pray for others. And to articulate daily thanks to God for all his blessings.

BUILDING BLOCKS

- Take time for your family to read together the Table of Duties from Luther's Small Catechism. Discuss the different roles God has given to us.

- Read 1 Corinthians 13, and then let members of the family choose a phrase from the reading that caught their attention. Listen to one another explain why that phrase became important.

- After reading a portion of Scripture, let each member of the family share the events of the day. After one person tells what happened, encourage the next one to summarize what was said. Other members of the family may be encouraged to respond as well. Create a prayer list from the events of the day, which can include reasons to thank God, and join hands in prayer after everyone has shared his or her story.

7. COMINGS AND GOINGS

Some finishing work, a few coats of paint, and your new home will be done. Your first guest already waits at your front door. *"Here I am!"* comes the gentle greeting. *"I stand at the door and knock. If anyone hears my voice and opens the door, I will come in and eat with him, and he with me"* (Revelation 3:20). The joy of his company will be multiplied many times over when you can unstrap your tool belt for the last time.

For now, step back and appreciate all the effort and sacrifice your home required. But don't imagine for a moment that you are the architect or that all the effort and sacrifice are entirely your own. Your spiritual home is the handiwork of the Lord God himself. All of it. You are his handiwork, and he is the great architect. He has shaped you and the other members of his household by his love and mercy.

Each of us is now a dwelling, fit to house the Lord of life himself. He has turned a house into a home. He has made you his by giving you faith. In your home he expects to find faith's fire burning brightly in the hearth.

How many times will the door open and close in your home? Someone knocks at the door and we open it. We welcome guests when they arrive and bid them farewell as they leave. The door opens. The door closes. Coming and going—that is what the Christian life is all about. The doorways of our lives are busy places. Warmed by God's enduring promises, we are ready to go out. There's work to be done. Seeds to be sown. Crops to be harvested. Then, filled with his love, we return to those we love in order to share our experiences, our joys, and our sorrows.

SHALOM

Hebrew is a difficult language to learn, but visitors to modern-day Israel quickly pick up a few phrases. By the end of the first day, every tourist knows at least one Hebrew expression: *shalom*. It means "peace."

Shalom is sort of a national greeting that can begin a conversation, renew an old acquaintance, serve as a blessing, or be directed heavenward in a prayer. It has a spiritual quality that conveys genuine well-wishing. Shalom, that is, may your day be filled with peace. Shalom! May you and I have a peaceful relationship. Shalom! May you find peace in your life.

Our visit to Jerusalem coincided with the city's third millennium celebration. Three thousand years have passed since David made this historic city his capital. Banners and posters everywhere invited us to "Pray for the peace of Jerusalem." Street vendors and cabbies greeted us in broken English with the same words: "Pray for the peace of Jerusalem." The familiar words struck a friendly cord. They were also sung by David himself (see Psalm 122). Then one remembers that David was also Israel's warrior-king. His hands were stained with the blood of his enemies. Given today's political landscape and the warfare thoughout the centuries, the word *peace* might have a hollow ring. But David meant a different peace.

The name Jerusalem is probably derived from the word *shalom*. It may once have meant "City of Peace." Yet this ancient holy city has changed political masters no less than 40 times in three thousand years. And now its people once again pray for peace.

Israel is a country surrounded, within and without, by enemies. In Jerusalem guns are visible on every street corner. Jerusalem itself is the prize. It stands as a sacred shrine to three major world religions—Judaism, Christianity, and Islam. A minor incident can touch off a new wave of bombings. A small shift in the political balance sends shivers of anxiety throughout the tense population.

Even to the untrained eye, it is obvious: there is no peace in Jerusalem. Nor has there ever been. Any hope for a real, long-term, lasting peace is tenuous at best. Where hatred rules, it can be no other way. In the City of Shalom, where visitors are invited to pray for peace, the contrast between man's idea of a real and lasting peace and God's becomes painfully apparent.

Peace is a precious thing. Every human who has been a victim of a fist raised in anger knows what it is to long for peace. Peace is still among the noblest of all human goals. And yet, for many, peace remains the most elusive of all human objectives.

> **Peace is among the noblest of human goals; and yet, for many, peace remains the most elusive of all human objectives.**

Peace among the nations of the earth is one thing. Peace under our own roofs is another thing. We desire them both. But there is a peace far more substantial, one that the unspiritual mind and the unbelieving heart cannot fully appreciate or even understand. The Christmas angel spoke of this peace to the shepherds watching their sheep near Bethlehem. The Prince of peace himself won this peace for us and for all people. He whispers at the door of our hearts: *"Peace I leave with you; my peace I give you. I do not give to you as the world gives. Do not let your hearts be troubled and do not be afraid"* (John 14:27). He reassures us that the war for our souls is over. He is the victor.

Blood has always been the cost of winning the peace. Men and women have shed their blood to secure peace for themselves and future generations. Blood was also the price for the peace we have with our heavenly Father. That was clear already in the Old

Testament when God designated bloody sacrifices to be offered by his people. The idea of blood-bought deliverance stretches back to Egypt and the Passover.

That Passover night air reeked of death. Huddled in their squalid little slave shacks, Hebrew families gathered and waited. They had picked clean the last meal they would ever eat in Egypt—a lamb, roasted and prepared with bitter herbs and spices. In the eerie darkness, they could hear the mournful shrieks of their Egyptian masters. The casualties of that awful night were being discovered one by one in Egyptian homes—every firstborn male slain by the invisible hand of divine justice.

But blood was also shed in Hebrew homes. It was the blood of a lamb, drained from the little animal's body and smeared on the lintels of their shanty doors. The angel of death passed over those homes with doorways decorated in blood. God's people were spared the ravages of the battlefield.

Like the freed Hebrew slaves of that first Passover, our night of terror is over. We too have been spared. God's holy Lamb has brought us peace. He has restored us to God's family. His lifeblood was poured out on the altar of God's justice in our place. He died on the battlefield so that we could live. His blood brought us out of our slavery to Satan and eliminated the tyranny of sin from our lives. His peace is the real and lasting peace that stretches out before us into eternity. Now a new homeland awaits. We are ready to live in God's presence. Nothing stands in the way.

We have good reason to celebrate. God's eternal peace rules in our hearts. It settles into our lives. It makes its way into our homes, where we are learning to live a new lifestyle—one that strives for unity and harmony and peace.

We Christians love peace. We work for peace. It still is among the noblest of all human goals. But we must never forget the peace we cherish most—the peace that surpasses all human understanding—God's eternal peace. That peace came at a very high price.

A LIFETIME ADVENTURE

General William Tecumseh Sherman was right: "War is hell." It carries a huge price tag. It tears humanity apart. In war humanity's most hateful instincts cut loose. Visit the Civil War battlefields at Shiloh or Gettysburg. Or go to Washington, D.C., and spend some time in the heavy air at the National Vietnam Veterans Memorial. Look at the faces of the people searching "the Wall" for the names of loved ones, comrades in battle, fallen heroes, sons and daughters, brothers and sisters, husbands and wives. You will be moved. You will see how war takes its terrible toll. It scars people for life.

The scars of family wars are just as ugly. If you doubt that, ask someone who has lived in a household where tyranny governs life's daily activity. Family members manipulate one another to gain control, to dominate, to enslave one another. Domestic conflict may not grab headlines in the same way that nuclear, chemical, or biological holocausts do, but they haunt people's souls in the same way, and they leave deep, permanent scars.

Many of today's families are literally disintegrating before our eyes. And it is happening in Christian homes as well. In some quarters of our society, family no longer provides the order it once did. In a very real sense, we are at war with ourselves. Or at least many of our families are. The times in which we live are truly precarious. When one of the pillars of social order crumbles, chaos cannot be far behind.

We are literally running out of time. The world in which we live is filled with people living in utter hopelessness. For some the pain in their lives is so deep that they are ready to discard life itself. For others the search for peace continues, but they do not know where to look. Domestic strife. Child abuse. Spousal abuse. Abuse of the aging. Family dissension and division. There's a horrible cancer eating its way into our families. The demise of so many families gives new urgency to every Christian's life.

This is our time to shine. People we spend time with every day—friends, relatives, colleagues, neighbors—are desperate. We stand at the crossroads of their lives. We have the answer—a real answer—a peace unequaled in human experience. Our mission is clear: reach out to the desperate with the gospel. Live as God's children. Shine like the stars of heaven. Be a beacon to a world at war, dying in sin. Show them the way out.

> **People we spend time with every day are desperate. We stand at the crossroads of their lives. We have the answer—a real answer—a peace unequaled in human experience.**

Our households share the message of Jesus when we are least expecting it. The world watches as our patience and generosity tell a story about Jesus. The neighbors listen as our conversations reflect God's love. We talk about Jesus without even thinking. Or we look with great care and planning for opportunities to tell someone of God's great love for him. Our faith is not just another part of our vocabulary. It permeates our being. The Lord Jesus guides our every thought, every behavior, every attitude, every word.

Moreover, this mission consumes us like some epic adventure. It is electric with daring and risk. We march in his army. We can afford to take chances. The battle plans are his. We cannot fail. In every conversation there is promise. In each new challenge, we rediscover the hope we hold so dear. He never sends us out ill-prepared or poorly equipped. He provides the energy to live as his children. He supplies the power to speak, the resources to do good, the desire to share our salvation with others, and the time we need to do his will. He is the God of peace, who works in us and through us to bring peace to the lost and dying.

Our comings and our goings have eternal purpose. And they are accompanied by the most reassuring of all promises. I AM is with us to bless our words and our efforts . . . as he always has been . . . as he always will be.

A GLANCE DOWN THE ROAD

The pain was not severe, more like pressure across my chest and down into my left arm. At a healthy 43, I was not thinking worst case scenario. But there I was, staring at a plastic model of a human heart, hearing a stranger tell me why bypass surgery was the only option. My wife and children stood by, helpless and in shock.

It's hard to predict how one will react when life takes an abrupt U-turn. I'm not very proud of my reaction. As far as I was concerned, my life was spinning wildly out of control. What's worse, my health crisis was quickly turning into a spiritual crisis.

As a husband and parent, I had always taken my family responsibilities seriously. As an educator I was good at managing the classroom. As a school administrator, I took pride in shaping curriculum and supervising the school's educational program. I made it my business to stay on top of developing issues—to be *in charge*. For all of my adult life, I had been in charge. Now suddenly everything, including life itself, was being ripped from my control.

Friends and relatives tried to cheer me. Clergymen came by to read Scripture. Cards poured in from church members, students, colleagues, wishing me well. They promised to keep me in their prayers. But my frame of mind did not improve. As the surgery date approached, I remember telling my wife, "I think I'm losing my faith."

An unsigned note tumbled out of a fistful of cards. I still don't know who sent it. Eight intrepid words were scrawled on it: *"Be still, and know that I am God"* (Psalm 46:10). Nothing anybody has ever said to me has ever meant more. Those eight words made me so ashamed. But in a heartbeat, my soul was lifted up, and I was soaring.

Some mortals get to know death's face more intimately than others. I consider myself doubly blessed to be among them. My encounter stirred up a new understanding in me: death is not abstract. It stalks you like some hunger-crazed beast of prey. Its hot breath had been on my neck for 43 years, and at the moment of my trouble, its teeth were beginning to sink in.

One day I would go out the door and not return to my earthly family. You hear that all your life. As a child I had prayed:

Now I lay me down to sleep.
I pray the Lord my soul to keep.
If I should die before I wake,
I pray the Lord my soul to take.

But death was always one of those relatively distant facts one comes to terms with *for other people.* Now, for the first time, I knew my death as a fact of *my* life.

My son, Paul, had a difficult time dealing with my health crisis. We are very close. In addition to a healthy father-son relationship, he had been my student for three years in a Lutheran elementary school. I knew he was searching to try to understand why God would put my life at risk. It was agonizing to watch. I was far more concerned about leaving my family in the lurch than anything else. His struggle made that possibility even more difficult to accept.

I certainly didn't have any answers. But I felt some kind of obligation to help Paul. After all, God gave us a family so that we might encourage one another on our way to heaven. I overheard myself telling him, "I've taught you how to play baseball and basketball, to love history and solve math problems. You learned to enjoy the woods and to hunt and fish from me. Maybe now God wants me to teach you how a Christian dies." The words caught me completely off guard. These were words of faith, so inconsistent with what I had been thinking and feeling. They took my breath away even as I said them.

I don't know what effect my little speech had on Paul. We've never talked about that conversation. He may not even remember it. But the words that came out of my mouth affected me deeply because they weren't my words. They were the words of God's Holy Spirit, intended for me to hear, as much as for my son. They were words sent for my comfort, to give me strength, to encourage me to hang on to Jesus in faith. They reminded me that I couldn't lose. If I survived and lived for a while longer to be a father to my children, a loving husband to my wife, a faithful servant in God's kingdom, I would be blessed far beyond anything I deserved. But if God wanted to take me to his heavenly home right now, that would also be in my best interest. My work on earth and all the suffering and pain of this life would be over. I couldn't even imagine all the glorious blessings that awaited me in that scenario. With either outcome I knew I would be living for my Savior.

> **This place we now call home is only temporary. The real prize still remains before us.**

This place we now call home is only temporary. The real prize still remains before us. Our future home in eternity will be well worth the wait. No more wars among nations or races. No more domestic strife. No more tears or pain or heartache or sadness. No more death or fear of dying. And no more fear of living either. We will be living with but one purpose: to give glory and honor and praise to God's righteous Lamb.

Our new home promises to be glorious beyond anything in our experience. It's what we have been waiting for! And even now it makes my heart pound with anticipation and joy just to think of it. It makes me want to celebrate even before I get there. Imagine, being with the Father, seeing his face without having to turn away in fear or shame! Imagine, living in the same house where the greatest hero of all time resides, having all the rights and privileges of membership in his family. Imagine, complete unity with every member of God's household. Mind-boggling, isn't it!

A builder's greatest obstacle is lack of imagination. Building projects take on some grotesque looks when blueprints haven't been carefully thought out: buildings without restrooms, upper floors without stairwells or elevators to get to them, rooms without entrances.

Our imagination has been impaired by the Fall. We may dream, but we still have a difficult time imagining the perfect home. That's to be expected. We have lived in an imperfect one all our lives. God gave a different dream to a few so that they might share it with us. None of them got to see the whole wonderful picture. But they did get to see fragments of what we can expect—our home for eternity.

The apostle John was one of the honored few. His inspired eyes saw what our impaired imagination could not. And, thankfully, what he saw, he described:

> I saw the Holy City, the new Jerusalem, coming
> down out of heaven from God, prepared as a bride
> beautifully dressed for her husband. And I heard a
> loud voice from the throne saying, "Now the dwelling
> of God is with men, and he will live with them. They
> will be his people, and God himself will be with them
> and be their God. He will wipe every tear from their
> eyes. There will be no more death or mourning or
> crying or pain, for the old order of things has passed
> away" (Revelation 21:2-4).

Each tired night before I go to sleep, I pray for the peace of Jerusalem to come to my house soon. And then I close my eyes . . . and wait. I know what I'm looking for. *Shalom.*

BUILDING OBJECTIVES:

- To value your eternal salvation more than anything else and teach the members of your family to do the same.

- To live the gospel in your daily family life and make use of every opportunity to tell others what Jesus means to you so that they too can have the same hope you have.

- To keep your earthly life in perspective by seeing heaven as your ultimate goal.

- To watch and wait with eager anticipation for eternity to begin. And to celebrate eternal life even while you remain on earth.

BUILDING BLOCKS

- Read Philippians 1:19-26. The apostle Paul was in prison awaiting his trial. He did not know whether he would live or die. Discuss what the passage means to each member of your family.

- Read Acts 20:13-36. This is Paul's farewell speech to the elders of the church at Ephesus. Discuss what he wanted these Christians to remember. What would you want each member of your family to know if you never saw them again? Share it.

- Read Psalm 121. Discuss how the Lord has blessed the coming and going of each family member.

- Jesus prepared his disciples before he left them. Read John 14:15-31. Discuss what Jesus promised would help his disciples after he left them. How do these blessings help us too?

THE KEYS TO LIFE
IN YOUR NEW HOME

1. Remind one another that God is really present in your daily family life. Receive the blessings of Holy Communion often, remembering all that Jesus has done for you. And encourage the other members of your family to receive the sacrament often.

2. Talk frequently about the blessings of the forgiveness of sins, salvation, and life in Jesus, blessings you enjoy through the miracle of Baptism. Celebrate these blessings.

3. Remain rooted in God's life-giving Word. Hear it. Study it together often. Apply it to life.

4. Practice Christian compassion. Minister to the needs of others.

5. Join together daily to worship God.

6. Communicate honestly, lovingly, and directly. Listen to one another with genuine concern. And talk with God often regarding your needs.

7. Remain focused on your heavenly goal. And, as you wait for eternity to begin, share the message of salvation in Christ Jesus with others at every opportunity.